TURBULENT TIMES & CLEAR SKIES

My Adventures in British Aviation

NAZIE EL MASRY

WITH JANE WARREN

MEREO
Cirencester

Mereo Books

1A The Wool Market Dyer Street Cirencester Gloucestershire GL7 2PR
An imprint of Memoirs Publishing www.mereobooks.com

Turbulent Times and Clear Skies: 978-1-86151-810-1

First published in Great Britain in 2017
by Mereo Books, an imprint of Memoirs Publishing

The address for Memoirs Publishing Group Limited can be found at
www.memoirspublishing.com

The Memoirs Publishing Group Ltd Reg. No. 7834348

The Memoirs Publishing Group supports both The Forest Stewardship Council®
(FSC®) and the PEFC® leading international forest-certification organisations. Our
books carrying both the FSC label and the PEFC® and are printed on FSC®-certified
paper. FSC® is the only forest-certification scheme supported by the leading
environmental organisations including Greenpeace. Our paper procurement policy
can be found at www.memoirspublishing.com/environment

Typeset in 11/17pt Century Schoolbook
by Wiltshire Associates Publisher Services Ltd. Printed and bound in Great Britain
by Printondemand-Worldwide, Peterborough PE2 6XD

This book is dedicated to my father,
for making me the man that I became

You only have to do a very few things right in your life, as long as you don't do too many things wrong

Warren Buffett

CONTENTS

PROLOGUE

❧

Amsterdam, 1986

Six seeds, pale green in colour.

Smaller than peppercorns they lay on Chencho's outstretched palm.

"What the hell are these?" I asked, curious.

"These are the beginning of your fortune," her husband Robbie replied, smiling.

I'd been sitting on our Chesterfield sofa, watching TV and smoking my pipe, when our maid Soad had answered the door a few minutes earlier. My best friend Robbie, who is Dutch, and Chencho, his Filipina wife, had arrived for an evening playing cards with me and Patricia.

Soad had welcomed them in.

"We got you a present," said Chencho when Patricia left the room for a moment. She was smiling.

Chencho and Robbie – with whom I worked at British Caledonian in Amsterdam – had just returned from a holiday in the Philippines. Patricia and I had travelled with them there before, but on this occasion we hadn't been able to go.

Chencho held up a small brown envelope.

"These are for your greenhouse," she declared, and tore it open. Pulling out a small wad of moist cotton wool, she peeled it back to reveal the six small seeds and showed them to me.

I laughed at the idea that these could build my fortune, but as a farmer's son I was curious to know what would emerge above the soil if I planted them in my small greenhouse.

A vegetable, or maybe a flower? I could not wait to find out.

The greenhouse, attached to our semi-detached house in an Amsterdam suburb, was my pride and joy. In a typically British way I grew cucumbers, tomatoes and courgettes – all from seed. Everything I planted grew, with the exception of peppers which didn't do well at all.

Chencho said I should germinate the little seeds in individual paper cups on a window sill, so I tucked them back in the envelope and left it in the kitchen for the evening while we played cards and enjoyed some drinks and dinner.

The following morning, after Patricia had gone out to her exercise class, I remembered the envelope. I went into the kitchen and asked Soad to bring me a small amount of earth. I wanted to see what would become of my magic beans.

We potted them up and left them on the window sill. After four days, five of the six pots had sprouted vigorous little green shoots which soared up several inches overnight. I called Chencho. "The seedlings are out of control."

"It's too warm, put them outside," she urged.

Patricia and I were about to go on holiday to Dallas for three weeks so I took the cups of seedlings out to the greenhouse in the side passage and asked Soad to look after them while we were away.

"Every day, just give them a little water, don't drown them, just a light spray," I instructed and urged her to leave the greenhouse door open so they wouldn't get too warm.

"Well, we'll see what happens," I thought to myself.

And boy, did those plants grow.

When we got back from holiday I was in for a massive shock. They were absolutely everywhere. One had smothered the tomato seedlings and the other had taken over the cucumbers, and these big leafy plants were all over the greenhouse. They were rampant, and as soon as I saw the leaves I knew exactly what they were.

While away, we'd telephoned Soad a couple of times and asked her, "How are things, how is the house?" Everything was fine, but she'd never mentioned anything about the marijuana plants taking over the green house...

When Patricia went out to cut a couple of cucumbers she wandered back into the kitchen, perplexed.

"Nazie, those plants; it's like the Day of the Triffids out there," she said.

She couldn't work it out at all, and I wasn't about to tell my saintly wife of eight years what I had ended up growing and why the cucumbers had been starved of light. But something had to be done, and soon. I phoned Chencho and asked her to call her friend Terry, who knew about these things. "Can you ask him what to do about these plants?" I begged.

Soon the message came back.

"Terry says, pick the petals, the top part of every plant, and put them in your humidor. Leave them for a while, and then you can smoke them," she explained.

I'm not one to waste time, I'm always full of action, so as soon as I heard this I plucked them all, and there were plenty – a whole jar of them. I picked up my

Sherlock Holmes humidor, shook out the tobacco, and stuffed it with the bright green tips; making sure I did all this well beneath the Patricia radar.

Next time Chencho and Robbie came around we were ready to go.

I stuffed my pipe and passed it to Chencho; she was a real pro. And soon we were laughing at any old silly thing. Life was wonderful.

This went on for a few weeks until one day when I came home and Soad took me to one side, well out of earshot of my 32-year-old wife.

"Mr Nazie," she said with a worried look on her face. "You better go and see your tobacco humidor."

"What's wrong?" I asked, as I dashed into the sitting room. I opened the humidor and it was empty. Arrggh. Patricia!

I ran into the kitchen.

"Why did you empty my humidor, Patricia?" I said, accosting her while she was chopping salad.

"Oh you had some tobacco in there that turned green so I threw it down the toilet," she said in her gentle but crisp Scottish lilt.

Patricia claims she couldn't work out why we were all so miserable the next time Robbie and Chencho came over to play cards. Apparently she had no idea that she'd thrown away thousands of guilders worth of the precious stuff.

There was no laughing; I swear, we cried for a month.

But for all that, Patricia did me a huge favour, of course. At the beginning of the greenhouse experiment my friends and I would share a puff and it was enough for us to end up laughing. But within a few weeks we were having a lot more than a few puffs each. And that is when I realised this is serious; that is when I discovered that the next day I felt empty. We used to laugh so much about silly things, but after a while you needed more and more to get the same effect, and this was always followed by an anti-climax.

So when Patricia threw the leaves away she also gave me relief. Temptation had been removed by my Scottish saint and I could see I was better off without it – after the crying! After crying came relief and that was the last time I smoked marijuana. I've never touched it since. Well, I've never had the opportunity, have I?

Chapter One

SWEET FANNY ADAMS

❧

*The starting point of all achievement
is desire – Napoleon Hill*

I must have been born with the ability to wheel and deal in my blood; I certainly didn't learn anything about business from my father. My mother Zahia was the smart one, but my father Ayad was the one who kept things in order and I was always in awe of him. He was a quiet, distinguished-looking man with a Charlie Chaplin moustache which was carefully dressed on a weekly basis by his barber. It had to be absolutely square. If one hair was out of order he would give the barber hell.

My father was a strict man and he understood the value of educating me. He was my champion and it was accepted in our family that I was his favourite. The sadness is that he left us before I had proved myself. I was just twenty-four when he died suddenly in 1967. His death definitely spurred me on to achieve something bigger. Ultimately, I think I wanted to prove that he had been right about me.

I was born during the war, on 3rd January 1943 in Cairo – 20 miles away from the pyramids at Giza and two months after the Battle of El Alamein.

My parents and family were delighted at my arrival shortly after the first major victory of the British Commonwealth forces over the German army. Success in the North African Campaign had been cause for celebration enough – historians believe that the battle was one of two major Allied victories that contributed to the eventual defeat of Nazi Germany – but for our family the arrival of another child, five years after my older brother Nabil, was nothing less than a happy mistake.

They had not intended to have more children after the births of Nabil and our sister Ragaa, two years his senior, but once they got used to the idea of me I was pampered and spoiled by everyone in our extended family.

We lived in a huge apartment with five bedrooms. Being wartime, I am told that there were shortages and sporadic air raids. However, I was too young to be troubled by them.

Instead, my life revolved around Fattheya, the wet-nurse who had had a baby around the same time as my mother and who had been employed to look after me, as was still the custom of middle-class Egyptian families during the war years.

I was two or three years old when Fattheya finally left us and I cried for a very long time. My new nanny was terribly strict, so I loved it when Fattheya used to visit and would sweep me into her arms.

In 1945, when the war ended, we went to Jerusalem and I was baptised in the Sea of Galilee where Jesus Christ was also baptised. My family like to tease me that this explains my subsequent success; when they do this I like to remind them that success certainly did not come very easily to me at all.

My grandfather was a very popular man who had arranged a senior administrative job at Egyptian National Railways, then still run by the British, for my graduate father. Egypt was the second country after the UK to have a railway system, after Robert

Stephenson had been contracted to build it in the late 19th century. But it appears that all my father did was go to his office, sign a few documents and have the rest of the day to himself.

This meant that my greatest delight as a little boy was going with my father to buy patisserie. We had a driver named Behnam who used to drive us downtown, but one day my father said to him, "Look, you don't have to drive us, we'll walk."

And in the late afternoon before my bedtime he took me by the hand and we walked to Groppie, a restaurant in the centre where they baked delicious cakes and beautiful gateaux.

This became a pattern for us. We would stroll there together, before eating a couple of choux à la crème – my favourite – and walking slowly back home, holding hands.

Walks with my Daddy were the best moments of my life; it was sheer delight, each step pure pleasure. He adored me and I loved him.

In 1948, after Palestine was taken over by the Israelis, everything changed for a while and there were no imports whatsoever into Egypt. I remember being given just half an apple in my lunchbox at this time because even they were suddenly so expensive. But when things returned to normal again my father was able to get a cook and to look after us in style once more.

The family fortune had been made by my great-grandfather, Mikhail Abu Dahre, who farmed cotton, maize and wheat on the river banks of the Nile in the south of the country.

It is said that if you stood on the River Nile, near the southern part of the city of El Fashn, he had land as far as the eye could see in three directions.

The land here is very fertile, particularly during the summer floods, and he was able to grow several crops each year. There was a citrus garden and in a good year he also managed a crop of hay to strengthen the ground.

Nicknamed 'the man with the strong back', my great-grandfather was so-called due to an incident that occurred in the mid-19th century before the British had seized control of Egypt.

In 1801, the Ottoman Sultan had sent his commander, Muhammed Ali, to Egypt in a final attempt to push the French army out of the country. Flushed with success, Muhammed Ali began consolidating his control over the Ottoman province of Egypt. But instead of remaining loyal to the Ottoman government in Istanbul, he wanted Egypt to break away so he could create a hereditary kingdom of his own and ultimately become the father of modern Egypt.

When Muhammed Ali's army marched south across the land a decade later, seizing land and confiscating grain from both peasants and the landed aristocracy, my great-grandfather's workers and farmhands fled and ran back to their houses to hide.

But my great-grandfather had just invested a great deal of money in acquiring from England a state-of-the-art threshing machine for processing wheat. He was so distraught at the prospect of leaving it behind in the fields to be plundered that he disconnected the motor from the main housing, before carrying it back to his farm house on his back; all the carts and horses had been taken by the fleeing farmhands.

It took him hours and hours in the burning heat to cross his land and because he had no water he was forced to drink his own urine to survive. When the other farmers discovered what he had done they were so impressed that they gave him a nickname that reflected both his determination and his strength.

But I'm sure that the man with a strong back would have been surprised by the way his eldest son – my grandfather – chose to share out his land in the years that followed. It is a story that explains why my surname is El Masry, not Abu Dahre.

My father was one of five sons borne to my grandfather and grandmother. When my eldest uncle got married my grandfather was so proud that he gave him half his estate. In Egyptian culture, the first-born son is highly valued.

His second son, my second-eldest uncle, received half what remained upon his marriage. The third uncle duly received half of the remainder, and so it went on. Unfortunately for him, my father – Ayad Demitry Abu Dahre – was the fifth son, and by the time he decided to get married my grandfather had passed away. And that is why, after he graduated, my father got sweet Fanny Adams.

The unfair division of his father's estate left such a bitter taste in his mouth that he wanted to sever himself from the family and decided to give his children his mother Soria's maiden name, El Masry, instead of his father's surname.

My grandmother came from a very wealthy family – in Egyptian, El Masry means 'the Egyptian' – and it is by the name of my grandmother's family that I have always been known.

Having said that, my father did inherit a certain amount of land and the income from that gave us a comfortable life in Cairo. We all went to private schools and enjoyed regular holidays. In the summers we would escape from the unbearable heat in the city and spend two months in Alexandria; San Stephano or Felougha in Lebanon; or at Miami Beach, Alexandria.

Our format was always the same, whatever the country; we would rent a house or a big apartment on the sea front so that Nabil, Ragaa and I could play in the sea from sunrise to sunset.

In 1952, when I was ten, Egypt became a republic after King Farouk abdicated. I was sheltered from the political changes, which didn't affect my life at all. Instead, I was much more bothered by the fact that when we moved to our elegant villa just outside Cairo, in the town of Heliopolis, my parents insisted that my brother Nabil and I should share a bedroom to pray together and work together.

Our home was beautiful, with antique French gilt Aubusson fabric upholstered chairs in the visitors' room and the classical furnishings to match, but while my parents were enjoying our new house, I was not.

We were part of Egypt's Christian minority and unfortunately my brother was terribly devout – he still is – so naturally, I didn't like this sharing one bit. Kneeling on the floor to recite the Lord's Prayer was very boring and it made my knees hurt. But my brother couldn't stop there, he would always keep going with long-winded thanks and worship. I just wanted to get it out of the way and go to bed.

I lack faith. For instance, sometimes I think that maybe Jesus's disciples rolled the stone. I know he was supposed to be risen after three days, but I always have this element of suspicion. You can see the problem.

We were also required to say grace before meals. Over the years, this developed into a very quick and painless prayer; thanking the Lord for health, strength, daily food and praising his name, Oh Lord Jesus Christ.

Then we could start eating. It was the easiest, shortest grace ever.

While Nabil followed his high-minded pursuits, my thing, basically, was sport. Action, teamwork, fun. At thirteen I was a squash champion and trained by a coach who thought I had talent. His name was Dardiri and after he left Egypt he became the national coach of the New Zealand squash team.

I was also captain of the basketball team, but because I was only 5'7" tall I dropped basketball and moved on to football. Soon I was captain of that too. I was a playboy in the making, not a monk. Everywhere I went I had friends, and I'm the same to this day.

I have always loved sport; it teaches you how to lose, as well as the value and importance of always getting back on to your feet and trying again when things don't work out. It's a lot more difficult to learn how to lose than to win, and knowing this has always given me a lot of satisfaction.

Academically, things were not so satisfying and I earned a reputation as the black sheep of the family. I didn't excel at school and was destined to become something of a horny bastard as a young man. But my predicament was made worse due to the fact that my older brother was always top of the class, as well as pious. My sister was clever, but laid back. As for me, I was only ever average; the 14th out of 28 students. But I did have a secret weapon – my photographic memory.

When I was four, I had started at the French Jesuit school – French is Egypt's second national language. My teacher was a nun and she was nothing short of a terror. She was very, very strict; No talking in corridors, staying in line, and so on. She used to hit us with a ruler on our knuckles if we spoke out of turn or were late to gym, or for any number of other reasons.

After three years my parents sent me to the English School in Cairo, run by Baptist deacons from the UK, which had an excellent reputation for sport and where I was taught in English rather than Arabic. I was to remain there, at times by the skin of my teeth, until I was sixteen. Some of the teachers were nice to the students, others not so nice, and I was certainly no angel at school. I had detention after detention.

However, if I had to play football on Saturday morning it was necessary to upgrade my detention to a 'caning of three strokes'. This I did not like, but I was centre-forward so my team kept on at me to make sure I swapped the detention for a caning, ensuring I could play. I had several of these damn things. Other boys made sure they were equipped with pads, books or even three layers of underwear, but the headmaster was no fool; if they were caught they got double strokes.

Instead, I devised another approach. After the first stroke I would sit up, hold my chest and pretend, very theatrically, that I was experiencing acute chest pain. I would then bravely resume the bending position and await the final two strokes. I discovered that following this technique the subsequent lashings were always very mild. I would then stand up, smile and say politely, "Thank you Sir".

But teachers weren't the only people who were allowed to hand out discipline at that time. Much worse was when I was disciplined by the head boy of a rival school, a Jewish teenager named Michel Chalhoub. I have never forgotten him for reasons that will soon become clear.

We had gone with our school football team to Victoria College, an English school in Alexandria, for our annual inter-school tournament. During the match, the host school's referee was favouring his own side and I got a bit carried away and loudly accused him of cheating. This did not go down very well with either the host team or their pompous head boy who had the authority, and temerity, to discipline children from visiting schools.

As soon as the half-time whistle sounded, Chalhoub called me into the changing room and walloped me three times with a gym shoe. I was not very amused to say the least but after the match, which we lost incidentally, the bastard acted as if nothing had happened. And from then on, whenever we crossed paths, he always tousled my hair, trying to be friendly.

I've never forgotten his name because in 1955 Michel Chalhoub converted to Islam in order to marry Egyptian actress Faten Hamama, and changed his name to Omar Sharif.

I never could hear a mention of Lawrence of Arabia, Doctor Zhivago or Funny Girl without thinking what a real son of a bitch he was.

During my final years at school I knuckled down finally and got ready for my O-levels. Sport was still very important to me but I was still not cowed by authority. On one occasion when I was captain of the basketball team, the PE teacher and I had an altercation about a field goal. I knew both my feet had been just beyond the three-point line when I scored, but he insisted one foot was inside the arc and called me out.

"It was valid," I shouted angrily, stopping play.

He strode towards me, looked me in the eyes and slapped me hard on the face.

Always a tightly-wound spring, I erupted in outrage. I started pummelling him and managed to get in several good punches before the other players stopped us.

After they had pulled me off him, he marched me into his office and called my father to report me for punching him. No mention was made of the slap he'd given me.

Later that night I gave my father the full story. He listened without comment and told me the teacher wanted to suspend me, despite my exams being so close.

The next day he came into school.

"Never lay a hand on my son again," my father said with ice-cold cool. "I don't hit my children and I do not permit a stranger to touch them either."

Following my father's intervention, we all shook hands and parted amicably.

At the age of sixteen I was able to join the prestigious Gezira Sporting Club, Egypt's pre-eminent sports facility. I showed a lot of promise in playing squash and won a couple of competitions. Soon, I had very little time for my studies.

"Forget it," my chemistry teacher told my sister Ragaa, who was by then studying at my school to be a teacher. "Nazie will never, ever pass these exams. He has no time for us, he hasn't done enough work."

Determined to prove him wrong, I spent the day before the exams reading my chemistry books. I got 90 per cent and what does my teacher say? "I knew it, I knew it, he's a very clever boy. I knew he was going to get top marks". It was like the political situation in America! The most important lesson I learned at school? The benefit of hindsight.

After O-levels, I set about enjoying my life as a junior playboy. Kissing and cuddling girls, staying out late with friends, and sport, sport, sport. If I wasn't playing squash I was playing table tennis, if I wasn't playing table tennis I was playing basketball, and so on.

Sex wise, I wasn't that involved as a youngster, but I was always out of the house; always busy with friends. My father found me infuriating. He would spend the morning reading his newspaper, and if the newspaper was not delivered all hell would break loose. If his wayward younger son was not back on time it was much the same story.

He always insisted I should be home by 2pm at the weekends, in time for lunch. But I was always late. It was always ten past two, or quarter past two, or sometimes half past two. He used to get very angry. He was a serious and austere man and he didn't understand my strong need for social interaction.

I was often late because of the lure of food. When I was downtown in Cairo there was a lovely little cafeteria that made wonderful snacks. My favourite was prawns with mayonnaise or a French dish – wait for it – boiled calves' brains with lemon juice. The chef would roll them in breadcrumbs and then fry them. And we used to eat them in a little piece of French bread. Of course I would lose track of time. I did try to be home at 2pm but it was very difficult for me with so many temptations on offer in the city.

Eventually my father decided it was time for me to knuckle down and it was then that he encouraged me to study Agricultural Engineering at Cairo University. I can tell you that I wasn't interested in this at all. I just wanted to enjoy life. So I took matters into my own hands at the interview he set up for me.

"Why do you want to study Agricultural Engineering?" the interviewer asked me quizzically, taking in my fashionable linen trousers and open-necked Egyptian cotton shirt at my university interview.

"Well, I really want to. Maybe I'll open a chicken farm," I said enthusiastically, omitting to mention that my father owned land and needed me to supervise operations for him.

Later, my father managed to speak to the interviewer to ask why I had not been accepted.

"I had hoped my son would look after my land in El Fashn," my father explained.

"Sir, he didn't mention anything about that," spluttered the interviewer. "He didn't mention you were a landowner, he just said he wanted to raise chickens."

My father was furious.

"What is going to happen to you?" he thundered. "What do you want to do with your life?" At least he had asked for my opinion.

"Well, actually, I'd like to apply to Vienna University to study industrial chemistry or go to London to study aeronautical engineering."

I could have done either; once I put my mind to something I enjoy doing whatever I have chosen to focus on. But I have to feel interested or it doesn't work.

I started German lessons, in preparation for the possibility of a new life in Vienna and applied to both institutions, rather hoping that neither would want me and I could carry on as before.

Acceptance of my place on the aeronautical engineering course at Chelsea College arrived three days before the letter from Vienna University, also offering me a place. So that was that. I was going to London to study. Had I not gone to the UK I would have gone to Vienna and had a completely different sort of life.

But as it was I found myself sitting on board a United Arab Airlines (now EgyptAir) Comet 4C, stuffed like a cabbage into one of the two tailored woollen suits my father had had made for me. I also had a beautiful new camel hair overcoat that went down to my knees. It was my first trip to London. I was seventeen years old. The date was 1st April 1960 which I thought was a terrific joke. I was wet behind the ears and had no idea about anything.

Fortunately, my father handed me all sorts of documents to read on the plane together with his firm invocation to "always look after your passport". There were notes about my allowance, and the address of a distant uncle on my mother's side, Air Commodore Youssef Wassef, who would be my guardian in London – very important as he would dispense my allowance on a monthly basis. Whenever I had a problem I was told to go to his office in Regent's Street and he would immediately sort things out for me.

Nothing had prepared me for the culture shock – and

the cold – of arriving in England's magnificent capital city at the start of spring; after I had managed to get out of the airport, that was.

I'd presented my passport and visa at immigration and was heading towards the train station at London Airport – as Heathrow was still called in 1960 – when I slid my hand into the pocket of my suit. No passport. Frantically, I ran back to the immigration counter and explained to the officer that I had lost it.

"I did leave it here," I insisted.

"Sir, I've been doing this for the last thirty years. I have never kept a passport and I'm not about to start now," he said in cultivated tones.

Feverishly, I searched my pockets – and found the damned thing in the pocket of the camel hair coat.

The immigration officer regarded the skinny, smartly dressed boy apologising profusely in front of him. "It's alright. Is it your first time here?" he asked.

"Yes," I said, pulling myself up to my full 5'7".

The first astonishing thing I noticed when I reached London and headed to the Egyptian Cultural and Education Bureau in Mayfair were the bikers in their leathers and head gear. I was used to bikers in Cairo wearing open shirts and little else.

The second astonishing thing was the magnificence of my destination.

Number 4 Chesterfield Gardens was an imposing five-storey Grade II listed building which had been the London residence of King Farouk, the penultimate king of Egypt, before his abdication in 1952 just eight years before my arrival in the city. It looked rather like a mini Harrods with its intricate stone façade and balconies, but was essentially just the student office for wet-behind-the-ears new arrivals in the city.

I identified myself and was relieved to be told that funds from my father had been received safely.

Soon I was speeding by taxi to east Putney to my new lodgings where I would live on a full-board basis. I rang the bell. One look at my landlady and I got the shivers. She was a big woman with a frightening bosom and with her hair tied in a bun at the back of her head.

She let me in and immediately started with the instructions; No smoking, eating or drinking in the room. Not that I was interested in any of that, but I was a bit annoyed to learn that no student visitors were allowed either. Then she showed me upstairs. The room was ice-cold, but she told me I could use the gas fire which was operated by a meter.

"You have to put shillings in this meter to put the heater on," she said, jabbing her finger towards the thing.

"Fine," I said. I popped in a couple of shillings. Once

the fire was on I was delighted with the heat. Unfortunately, the shillings did not last very long. Every ten minutes I had to get out of bed shivering, and feed the thing. I was destined to spend a fortune trying to keep that room warm.

Another interesting feature was the bathroom. I was not interested in sitting in half a bathtub of tepid water so I used the shower over the bath and dried off in front of the gas fire.

As for the meals she served up every day, they were boiled disasters and worse than hospital food. I began to realise how spoiled I had been in Cairo. But the one good thing was that my landlady always had a lot of change. I certainly needed it to feed her damned meter.

Considering I had never lived on my own before, none of this was a particularly pleasant introduction to my new life in London.

I lasted three weeks before I moved into a bedsit at 99 Philbeach Gardens, a Victorian terrace in Earls Court, with a friend from college.

College was great. I may have been a mediocre student in Cairo, but I excelled at college and enjoyed most subjects with the exception of metallurgy — metals, metals and more metals. They all looked the same to me with or without their carbon content, I never could tell. But I passed my chemistry A-level with flying colours as soon as I arrived in the UK. A year later I took my physics A-level and in 1963 I passed engineering drawing. This was a concession by Chelsea College for foreign students; we could sit our A-levels at a later date.

When I wasn't studying I was listening to the Beatles, The Rolling Stones, Cilla Black, or hanging out at my local disco, the Les Chelles club in Earls Court. What a time to be in London.

Chapter Two

A GIRL IN THIGH-HIGH BOOTS

❧

*The starting point of all achievement
is desire – Napoleon Hill*

As soon as I arrived in London, the lager-and-lime cocktail replaced the squash racket. I was a hedonist, hell-bent on enjoying the start of the swinging Sixties, including the girls in their miniskirts.

After visiting my family in Egypt in the summer break, I moved to 40 Kensington Gate, an apartment owned by a Baroness, with an Iraqi friend, Walid Ayoub, and a Jordanian boy named Adnan, both of whom were a lot better off than me.

I was a war baby, born to a middle-class family in Cairo on 3rd January 1943. I wasn't planned but I was very much loved, especially by my father; I was to become his favourite.

My family in 1947: My mother Zahia and my father Ayad with his distinctive moustache. Behind him *(left to right)* are my brother Nabil looking like a cocky little s**t, me, and our sister Ragaa.

I was seven years younger than my sister Ragaa and five years younger than Nabil, my brother. There is already a naughty gleam in my eye shortly after I started school at the age of five.

This photo of my parents, Zahia and Ayad, was taken in El Fashn, Upper Egypt. My mother always took a good photograph and even my father seems relaxed here. He was devoted to her.

On holiday visiting our family in El Fashn, Upper Egypt. I borrowed the fez from the maintenance guy at the family apartments.

The English School in Cairo where we were taught by Baptist deacons from the UK and where I received detention after detention. I am the short cocky boy (*centre of the back row*) with folded arms.

Aged 14, with my mother and my father - who is already beginning to look worried about the future prospects of his fun-loving youngest son.

I'd just learned to fly a Tiger Moth at Biggin Hill Airport in South London, where I was studying the practical part of my aeronautical degree. My friend Nouradine Walgi *(left)* and I look very proud of ourselves.

In the cockpit of a BAC 1-11-200 at Gatwick, shortly after I got my first job with British United Airlines in 1965, at the age of 22. The red collar signifies my status as a Junior Licensed Technician.

My brother Nabil and I on a hotel balcony in Beirut, Lebanon, in 1963. He was at a medical conference and I'd jumped on a flight to see him - and picked up some cigars en route. We are very different but in recent years have become close.

With British United Airlines in 1965: I had 'soft' hands so I was made a supervisor, not a mechanic, and that meant I got to wear a BUA uniform.

Proud Daddy: With Ferdy, outside our home in Horley, in 1968, when he was nearly a year old, and shortly before I set up my first business, Auto Line.

Samantha and Ferdinand at our home in Libya. Ferdy was always a very protective older brother.

Mr Horny Bastard with his pipe and shades in Tripoli. I was in uniform but never put epaulettes on my shirt because I never cared for them.

With my best friend Robbie's wife Chencho in a forest near Haarlem, Holland, in the mid-1970s. We were all enjoying an autumnal barbeque when the police arrived and told us to extinguish it due to the risk of starting a fire in the dry leaves. Our food was rather undercooked, but we still ate it.

The day a British Caledonian BAC 1-11 veered off the runway into the mud at Schiphol airport, Amsterdam. It took 48 hours to extract the aircraft, but first the handlers had to remove the passengers' luggage.

Patricia at the British Caledonian ticket desk at Amsterdam's Schiphol airport in 1975. The first time I met her I pinched her bottom.

With Patricia on our wedding day on 14th July 1978, in St Petersburg, Florida. My Scottish bride was 24; I was 35.

Valetta, our four-bedroom Tudor house in Horley, West Sussex, where we met George the ghost.

Amsterdam, 1979: Here, I am trying to work out why one of the engines on this DC10 is not producing power. As a line maintenance engineer, my job was all about trouble-shooting and I enjoyed the adrenalin-rush tremendously.

My mentor and my boss: Arnold Sheead *(right)* gave me my first job in 1965, when I was 22. I was to work for the Yorkshireman for the next 25 years; all the way from BUA, to British Caledonian and then, in 1987, to British Airways – two years after this photograph was taken at the retirement party for instrument engineer Pete Lucas in 1985. © The family of Pete Lucas.

The house where it all began: In 1982, Julian was born and we set up Fersam in the cellar of Gaaistraat 14, near Amsterdam. Space was so tight Patricia had to sit on the stairs near the wine rack to operate the telex machine.

Proud father: I could have had a thousand more Julians.

Embarking on a flight from Amsterdam to Gatwick on a BAC 1-11-500 with Patricia and Julian in the early-1980s. This was the same model of plane on which I had put out a fire en route to Amsterdam a few years earlier.

My elder sister Ragaa visiting me in the mid-1980s in Amsterdam. She visits every couple of years.

I love food and I love cooking. This photo was taken in America where we were visiting family. I'm allergic to prawns now.

Dr Sabel's surgery in Holland; on the right was the entrance to our office, on the left the entrance to our home.

With my best friend Robbie in the garden of Frisolaan 10, our house in Holland. We used to play tennis a couple of times a week on the court I built in the garden.

There can't be too many
aeronautical engineers who have
starred as Mr April!

With my sister-in-law Alice *(left)*,
shortly before I rode a camel for the
first and last time.

With Julian in 1987, when he was five. Unfortunately, the camel leaked
from both ends.

My most senior position: As British Airway's Station Maintenance Manager in Amsterdam, shortly before I took early retirement in 1988 at the age of 45. The four stripes on my wrist are topped with a violet letter 'E' to show I am an engineer not a pilot.

Fun with Julian and my brother, Dr Nabil Ayad El Masry *(right)*, shortly before I left British Airways in 1988 at the age of 45. I had already been working long hours to establish Fersam.

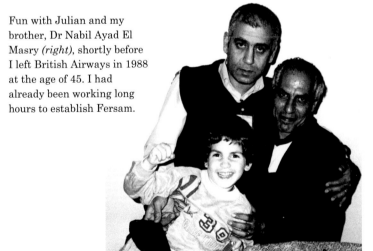

I smoked a pipe until I was 50, when I developed asthma. This photo was taken in Holland, a few years after I took early retirement from BA.

In the late 1980s, I flew first class to Egypt using free tickets from one of the airlines I supplied, hoping to do business with EgyptAir. This photo was taken with my friend, Ashraf, at the El Gezira Sheraton on the River Nile as I tried a hubbly-bubbly for the first time; I drew so much I nearly passed out.

In addition to my £60 a month allowance, my father also gave me a clothing allowance twice a year of £28 which I spent with my friends on beer; it was never used to buy clothes. At the beginning of every month we students lived well, but as the month went on we ate bread and butter at worst, or a cheese roll at best, until 'pay day'.

From time to time, my father used to send people to check on me. Sometimes I was taken out for dinner by a senior engineer from EgyptAir, Mohsin Faradin, whom my father had asked to keep an eye on his son.

Mohsin was in his mid-forties, a very good looking guy, and clearly didn't want to spend too much of his evening with me. He used to come to see me with his little dolly bird, take me out for a steak, and at the end he would give me £5 and 200 Lucky Strike cigarettes. Throughout the meal I could see his girlfriend playing with his legs under the table. He was kind enough to take me out but clearly wanted me to hurry up.

As for me, a particular girl had also caught my eye.

Carmen was a good looking Spanish girl whom I had seen a few times at the Les Chelles club. One night, she was being circled by some rich Iraqi boys with fast cars who seemed a bit enthusiastic. One of them wanted to take her home with him but I was not very comfortable with the situation because he had a bad reputation and I feared for her safety. So I walked calmly towards her and quietly warned her.

"Oh, rubbish," she declared, and started laughing her head off.

"Really, you better go home now," I gently insisted. She continued laughing, but she and her friend sensibly made their way home alone.

It's a good thing too, because she was destined to become the mother of my eldest two children.

We had a short relationship that summer, but when she returned to Spain for a while I was once again young, free and single in town, and I set about having a good time.

However, before Carmen left she helped teach me an important lesson. Adnan was a very big gambler who played poker from Friday night until Sunday morning with a group of student friends. I joined them sometimes, but I was not very lucky. Naturally, this inspired me to try to develop a winning system.

Adel Ibrahim Mina Makkar, my best friend from school in Cairo, was also studying in London. One day he and I went to a gambling place in Swiss Cottage and carefully studied the roulette wheel. We noticed that the middle dozen numbers, 13 to 24, came up every few spins. One night, after receiving my allowance, we decided to go for it; gambling gradually and increasing the funds to cover the previous losses.

At the beginning we started out well. We had great

dreams of what we were going to do with the winnings. But then we started to lose. Carmen was a lot wiser than we were and kept on praying that we would continue to lose in order that we would learn a lesson. But we couldn't stop.

As the evening wore on, we put in every last penny we had in a desperate bid to recoup our money. The wheel spun, and spun again. But no sign of the middle dozen. This went on for no less than seventeen spins of the wheel. This had never happened during our careful study of the roulette table.

The final indignity came when we had to walk home as my VW Beetle had run out of petrol; I had no money left to fill her up. The law of averages let us down, but the experience was – as Carmen had hoped – a memorable lesson.

I could not afford the Kensington apartment after Walid and Adnan returned home to Iraq and Jordan, so I moved back to Philbeach Gardens and this time took the ground floor bedsit at number 30.

One night, my Malaysian friend Lim Pee Hong, who was studying mechanical engineering, was cooking us chicken and rice for dinner. Lim was a good cook and the deal was that I bought the food and he cooked it for us.

Just as we started to eat there was a tap on the

window. Outside, was a young woman with red hair and blue eyes who had lost her key and was locked out. I let her into the building, leaving my bedsit door slightly ajar. The smell of our delicious meal wafted into the hallway as she explained, in her attractive Irish lilt, that she would wait there for her flat-mate to arrive with a key. It was impolite not to ask if she had eaten. Surprisingly, she replied that she was very hungry, so I cut up my half of the chicken and shared the rice. She loved it, and when her girlfriend arrived they went upstairs to her place.

A few days later came another tap on my bay window. It was Joyce, the Irish girl. I let her in and she walked across the room and placed a five pound note on my mantelpiece.

"The other day when you shared your meal with me, I was starving and really appreciated sharing your dinner. I insist we go out for a meal of your choice," she explained with a beguiling smile. Initially I refused, but she convinced me she was serious. We had dinner together at the Sarabia Restaurant in South Kensington, opposite the underground. Afterwards we went back to my room and got to know each other much, much better.

This carried on for a few weeks and I really adored her, but our relationship was confusing. Sometimes she would hang around for two or three days.

Sometimes she would excuse herself for the evening and explain that she had to go to work. At other times she would disappear for a number of days. There were even occasions when a limousine would turn up for her and the driver would wait for her to get changed, before whisking her away – I knew not where. Her work was a bit of a mystery, to say the least.

When I asked her where she was going she said she worked in a nightclub and had special guests to entertain. Still very young and naïve, I assumed she must be a hostess in one of the night clubs.

Then one day she tapped on the window as usual. I let her in and we embraced and were close. Afterwards, she dissolved in floods of tears and told me that I should find someone else as she was leaving her job, London, and me, and would never be coming back. I quizzed her and she mumbled something about looking after some men, shopping, cooking and making the tea for them. She also mentioned that she was going to have to change her identity for good. I was devastated when she ran out of the flat and disappeared.

The following day her bedsit was empty. When I asked her girlfriend where she had gone, she told me Joyce was a high class call girl with some very influential clients.

Two days later a Royal Mail train heading from Glasgow to London in the early hours of Thursday, 8th August 1963, was attacked by a fifteen-strong gang of robbers who had tampered with the line signals. Led by Bruce Reynolds, and assisted by Buster Edwards and Ronnie Biggs, among others, they stole £2.6 million (equivalent to £49 million today). The bulk of the stolen money was never recovered. This incident is, of course, known universally as the Great Train Robbery.

Following hints from her friends, we all concluded to our distress that Joyce had been hired to look after the gang.

Five days after the robbery, police discovered evidence that the gang had used Leatherslade Farm, near Oakley, Buckinghamshire, as a hideout.

The farm was deserted but the police found a large quantity of food, bedding, sleeping bags and a Monopoly board game. Most of the gang were eventually arrested and convicted, but Joyce was not heard of again, although the mastermind of the operation – Gordon Goody – sued the People newspaper from prison for suggesting he had "coerced an innocent and decent young woman" into taking part in the robbery. One of the detectives on the case described Goody as the "brilliant quartermaster" who ensured that all the equipment, vehicles and personnel were in place.

He won the case and received £2 in damages. Was his "innocent and decent young woman" Joyce? I have always wondered.

Forgetting her was difficult. Her disappearance was a great loss and we never spoke again. It was a very sad affair. My parents even sent me a ticket home to recover from the relationship for a few weeks.

Later in my college years I rented a bedsit at 58 Onslow Gardens, South Kensington. I knew my landlord was Polish but it wasn't until he died that I discovered he had been the notorious slum landlord, Peter Rachman, whose name lives on as a byword for the sort of rogue landlord who mends broken windows with cardboard instead of glass. Rachman was worth a great deal of money, much of which he kept under his mattress. And he needed sex every afternoon as part of his working day. But he was also a very private person and kept well to himself.

By the time I was living in one of his properties he had largely moved out of slum-landlording into property development and had installed a Polish housekeeper in the basement of number 58 to keep the place clean.

One day, two years after I arrived in London, this housekeeper told us that our landlord had died of a heart attack.

It wasn't until the Profumo Affair hit the headlines the year after his death, that it emerged both Christine Keeler and Mandy Rice-Davies had been his girlfriends, but the fact that our landlord had been seeing Rice-Davies was no secret to us.

I was living in the second floor bedsit, but the largest room in the house, the prime front-room bedsit, was home to Mandy – which was understandable, given their relationship.

We knew our landlord was her boyfriend; I saw him at the property several times. Rachman was a stocky man, not very tall, who wore thick-rimmed glasses. But never mind him; we all enjoyed watching Mandy.

"There's this girl sitting in the front room and she's wearing thigh-high boots and no underwear," one of my friends said breathlessly one evening after he'd run upstairs to my flat to give me the news.

We dashed back downstairs, ran into the street and sure enough, there were visual riches for us teenagers to enjoy.

Mandy was wearing thigh-high boots and standing in her front room slowly smoking a cigarette. When she saw us strolling back and forth outside, she sat down on a chair in the bay window and slowly crossed and uncrossed her legs, taking pleasure in exhibiting herself. She loved the fact she had our attention.

From that point on all my college friends made a

point of coming over regularly to view the evening show. We never spoke to her, but she seemed to love the attention.

These were fun times, as was the Christmas tradition that saw some of us Chelsea College boys jumping from the Serpentine Bridge into the freezing waters of the forty-acre lake in Hyde Park. Landing in fairly shallow water amid weeds and duck poop was one way to have a quick dip. I did this for a few years until I caught a terrible cold and vowed never to do it again.

My first experience in business came in 1964, three days before my final exam. My exams had gone well with the exception of the dreaded metallurgy, which I had to re-sit. I couldn't even tell stainless steel from mild steel; I hated the subject. And I wasn't the only one. My former flat-mate, Lim Pee Hong was just as confused, and there were a few others too. Something had to be done so we decided we needed to ask one of the junior professors for extra lessons. The only problem was that we were due to retake the exam in less than a week.

We drew straws as to who would ask for the lessons and I need not tell you who picked the short straw.

I walked into my professor's office, very nervously, and asked him if we could have some private lessons and how much they might cost.

"You come in three days before the final exam and ask me for lessons?" he said, amused.

"Well, is there anything you can do for me? I just want to pass the exam because it's hindering my graduation," I explained.

He laughed and told me to go and see him the following day with £20. It was the end of the month and that was a lot of money; a third of my monthly allowance. But I had a plan. I went to the other students and sold them quarter shares of the deal for £5 each. I returned the next day with the £20. The professor was smart; The test contained eight questions and in exchange for the money he gave me just five of them.

"You try and answer these and we'll see what you can do," he suggested.

But even with open books and the questions in front of us we had a job to pass. I scraped through with 53 per cent, the others with similar scores.

But something much more significant had happened. I had made my first business deal. Was it satisfying? It was exhilarating.

Chapter Three

DRIVING SIR FREDDIE

❧

The real secret of success is enthusiasm –
Walter Chrysler

Some things work, others don't, but there is always something to be learned from every experience. I discovered this the hard way; by making my own mistakes and by always developing from those mistakes.

If you do a deal, the secret is always to remain on your guard. After being disappointed so many times I have to double-check that nothing is going to fail. When I say something I mean it, but not everyone is like that. I'm not a pessimist, but I'm a calculating optimist. I love to leap, but I always look first.

And I always have a back-up plan. I make provisions because you always need an alternative to fall back on. And if I make a mistake, I don't blame anybody; I just sulk for a little while and I move on.

It was a great feeling passing all my exams, even the vexed metallurgy. I hired graduation robes for my graduation ceremony which was held on a hot summer's day in July 1964 in Chelsea Town Hall on the famous King's Road. My family were delighted with my success and my father assumed I would now return to Cairo.

My guardian in London, Air Commodore Youssef Wassef, promised to get me an engineering job with United Arab Airlines (now EgyptAir), the flag carrier airline of Egypt for whom he worked. In London he was the airline's overseas representative, paid to lubricate the wheels of big aircraft contracts while distributing what we might call 'the sugar lumps' when the deals were done.

During my college years I had spent many hours studying the practical side of aeronautical engineering at Biggin Hill Airport in South London, and my uncle knew how much I had enjoyed it.

It wasn't like work, I found it fun, even though I had

'soft' hands and always found the tools difficult to handle – a deficiency that was to remain with me for the rest of my career. But I went on to become an engineer, not a mechanic, so it wasn't a problem because once you got a job as an engineering inspector and supervisor you weren't allowed to touch any tools; that was the job of the airframe mechanics, the engine boys and the fitters. If an engineer like me was to pick up so much as a wrench the unions would down tools immediately. My job was to use my knowledge to run the teams who did get their hands dirty.

I had always been interested in flying and while I was training at Biggin Hill I made time to get my pilot's licence on a Tiger Moth, but following the death of one of our relatives in a flying accident my father didn't want me to have anything to do with flying. He even threatened to stop my allowance if I continued with it.

I suppose flying at that time wasn't a particularly safe thing to do. His cousin's son, Nabil Tadros, was doing 'circuits and bumps' in a twin-engine high-wing Russian Antonov during crew training when he died; this is when a pilot intentionally touches down and immediately goes up again. But Tadros overshot, went up, banked too hard and the plane went down. Since that day my father wanted me to have nothing to do with it. "There will be no flying," he declared.

However, he still continued to hope that I would agree to manage our farmland in the south of Egypt. Naturally, I had other ideas.

At the exciting age of twenty and with all my friends around me in London, I wanted to stay in the swinging capital little longer. Even though I was still living on the allowance from my father I was not keen on returning to Egypt right away because my Spanish girlfriend had returned to London. At a sophisticated twenty-seven years old, Carmen was five years my senior which didn't trouble me at all because she was a very good Spanish cook; and everyone knows that the easiest way to a man's heart is via his stomach.

We went dancing, had a good time and even went on holiday to Ibiza. Gradually I got serious about her. She was confident and loved outdoor activities – we spent most of our free time in the open air. Some of my friends thought she was too old for me, but the age gap didn't bother me at all. We had fun.

After a while she got a job in a cafeteria near Smithfield market so she could stay in London and we could continue our relationship.

It was in Smithfield market that I learned about meat, as well as an important business lesson that was to remain with me from that point on.

In order to buy meat at the market you need to get

up very early. Trading starts at 2am, by 6am everything is sold out and by 7am the market is closed, so I would arrive before 5am when there was still meat on sale.

I used to buy three or four lambs for the freezer, at prices you could never dream of finding in a supermarket.

The first time I did it I felt very proud of my haul. Each lamb had been butchered and wrapped in muslin cloth, and I placed the carcasses in the boot of my car. It was only when I was home and pulled off the muslin to get them ready for the freezer, that I saw what I had bought.

Have you ever seen a three-legged lamb? Neither had I, until the day I did my first deal at Smithfield market. Not only that, but as well as only three legs, there were only two shoulders.

I was shocked. I went back the following week and mentioned it to the chief in charge of the market. He just laughed and explained that this was the inauguration of the relationship. From that day on they always gave me fairly good deals. As for me, I got smarter, less green, and learned to keep a close eye on my purchases. Never believe what someone tells you; always check it for yourself.

There were a couple of guys at the market whom I got to know and came to trust. One of them asked me to buy cigarettes for him when I next went abroad. He paid me, but he also taught me about meat. He showed me how to tell if meat is tender by digging your little finger into the flesh to see if it is soft and smooth. And also to look for cuts without too many veins. This is information I have never forgotten.

Although Carmen and I had never lived together, on 18th December 1965, we got married.

We had a small party at Carmen's flat for a few friends; she had been living with two other girls in Maida Vale, near the Edgware Road. The sole representative from my family was Uncle Youssef, who attended the brief wedding with his family.

I respected my uncle absolutely. He had made life so much easier for me in London. He had helped me open a bank account when I had first arrived in London and ensured that every month the £60 from my father was waiting there for me. He also helped me get my Egyptian passport renewed every seven years until his death – passport renewal outside Cairo is normally required every five years.

But as well as oiling the wheels of my life in London, he had also been very strict with me for "my own good" as he put it. He was very easy-going with his son, my cousin Kamel, but whenever I wanted to do anything he would always raise objections with the phrase, "I'll think about it," which always meant no. Because of this I held him the highest esteem and I can see now that he was probably right.

It was only after our wedding that I wrote to my father telling him about the ceremony, with the words, "By the time you receive this letter I will be married".

His reaction was very cool and he did not express any opinion, which I knew meant he definitely was not amused.

When I left Cairo I had promised to write to him every week and he promised to do the same. However, my father insisted I wrote to him in Arabic. Having studied at an English school I was allergic to Arabic, but when I left Cairo I had promised I would write to him in Arabic to improve it. Unfortunately, I was a bit lazy in complying and only managed a few sentences every now and then. My father, however, stuck to his word resolutely and wrote to me at least three times a month while I was in London.

I loved his letters. He would write stories about what he did went he went to town, and about how he would think of me every time he passed Groppie, the French restaurant where we used to buy the patisseries together when I was a little boy.

I was told by another family member that when my father walked past Groppie he would have tears in his eyes. I used to love reading his letters; he always made me feel that I was part of him still.

He would give a good tip to the postman when he delivered a letter from me, so all the postmen were very anxious to deliver my mail. And sometimes he even used to call me on the radio – he had a friend who worked for the Egyptian Broadcasting Corporation, the EBC, who would arrange an open line so my father and I could talk to one another, which was nice.

Carmen and I rented an apartment in Streatham Hill, an hour's easy commute south down the old A23 to London's Gatwick Airport – an important fact, because I was now a professional aeronautical engineer.

Just a few months before my wedding, Freddie Laker – later, Sir Freddie – had given me my first job. At the time, he was Managing Director of British United Airways (BUA) and had made the news headlines because he had just changed the entire face and future of British aviation.

Until then, BUA had been an independent airline which, like other independents, only did charter work. In BUA's case, they also had a contract with the Ministry of Defence to move troops to and from Germany.

With his Rolls-Royce and his string of race horses Freddie was destined to become a serious player in the

British aviation industry, but at that time BUA was a fledgling compared to the national carriers and Freddie was still an ambitious man desperate to gain entry into an industry which, in the late 1950s, was still controlled by state-owned British European Airways (BEA) and British Overseas Airways Cooperation (BOAC). Being a private enterprise, BUA had had very little chance to compete.

But in 1960, just after I gained my aeronautical engineering degree, everything changed when the Civil Aviation Act opened up an array of new routes and BUA moved swiftly to apply for licences for more than twenty of them.

Everyone thinks it was all Freddie, but they forget that back then he was under the thumb of Group Captain Loel Guinness, an heir of the famous banking family and a former RAF Second World War wing commander who had been MP for Bath in the 1930s and early 1940s.

Guinness was President of BUA and owned ten per cent of the airline; Laker was his Managing Director. Every time they met they would row and that was to prove one of the catalysts that led Freddie to eventually leave and set up his own airline.

But that came later.

As soon as Laker heard through the grapevine that

BUA was going to be awarded some of the highly prized and lucrative European, African and South American routes, he celebrated his success by ordering a whole new fleet of aircraft. His victory roll totalled twenty-two BAC 1-11s 200s and 500s and four Vickers VC10s – Britain's new rival to Boeing's 707 – at a total cost of nearly £20 million.

Watching the evening news, and seeing Freddie standing on the ramp guiding aircraft to the stand during the bulletin, made me more determined than ever to stay on in the UK and not return to Cairo. Exciting things were happening here.

I phoned Uncle Youssef, who by now had a diplomatic position at the Egyptian Embassy in London, and told him I needed engineering experience before returning to Egypt. Very kindly, he spoke to his friend Ivor Gregory, the chief maintenance engineer of BEA.

The upshot was that I found myself en route to BEA's training centre to take a course on the Vickers Viscount – the first turboprop airliner in the world. British-made, it had four propeller engines but to the casual observer looked a bit like the sleek Boeing 737s jet planes that would be introduced in 1968. Most of the other engineers on the course had come out of the Air Force and were much older than me. I was fresh out of college and got top marks relying on my photographic memory and high degree of motivation.

However, there was a hitch in going to work for BEA immediately because of the question of my nationality. The trade union, the Association of Licensed Aircraft Engineers, insisted that I had to be naturalised first, but I was told the paperwork would take weeks.

I could not afford to wait and was determined to stand on my own two feet as an independent adult.

Ivor Gregory called his friend, the chief engineer of Laker's BUA, Mr Arnold Sheead. Gregory knew Sheead was desperate for licensed junior engineers because of a row that had erupted about pay and conditions. Freddie was a tycoon in the style of Donald Trump; if he was not happy with any of the employees, he would fire the lot.

And that's just what he had done – an event that had also made it onto national television. Consequently, BUA were taking on new engineers to plug the gap.

I got an interview immediately. When I arrived at Arnold Sheead's office the gruff, bespectacled Yorkshireman was surprised by how young I was.

"Show me your palms, lad," he said with a laugh.

I held up my hands. "Humph," he snorted. "Most of my engineers are ex-RAF. We don't like pen-pushing engineers from college."

I left his office confused and asked his secretary what would happen next.

She came back with multiple forms and a message from chief Sheead; I would begin work as a junior licensed technician on Monday and should expect rapid promotion.

I was the first of a new wave of graduate engineers who would gradually take over from the older RAF engineers, many of whom seemed to be senior citizens to me, although I think they were probably not older than their early forties. Generously, they were very tolerant with this new young upstart and I'm grateful for all they taught me.

In all, I was destined to stay on the payroll of that organisation, and work under Arnold Sheead, for twenty-five years while it went through various mergers, from BUA, to British Caledonian and eventually, in 1987, to British Airways – the world's flagship airline.

Apparently, Arnold Sheead even discussed the issue of my Egyptian nationality with Freddie Laker and assured him I would get my British paperwork the following month.

As soon as I graduated I wrote to my father to tell him that I was no longer in need of an allowance. A few months after that I became a dual citizen of Egypt and the United Kingdom.

From that point on my life was my own and everything that followed came from hard work, determination and a sheer bloody-mindedness to keep going, even when the chips were down.

I was now working for BUA's line maintenance division, the front line of a £2.9 million-a-year engineering department.

Line maintenance engineers must have an ability to react instantly to unforeseen circumstances, diagnosing and rectifying fault with aircraft and carrying out the basic daily checks that need to be made within their normal turnaround time.

The basic aim was to keep BUA's fleet safe and ready to fly. The heavier checks were carried out by my colleagues in the base maintenance division and would usually involve taking the aircraft out of service.

My salary seemed good, it was certainly more than my allowance and I was quite satisfied until one day, six months into the job, when one of my favourite mechanics, Jim Williams – a shop steward for our union – found out exactly how much what I was earning.

"Nazie, have you got a minute?" said Jim, while I was sitting in the office at lunchtime. "Is this your salary?" he asked, flipping over my monthly payslip.

"Yes," I replied.

Well, they almost went on strike over it. It turned out I was getting less than the air frame fitters, the engine men and the mechanics.

Jim marched into Arnold Sheead.

"If something isn't done, we're going to go on strike for Nazie because they're using him as a slave," boomed Jim.

This was threat enough to get my salary doubled. This was a very handsome increase and the figure was back-dated from the beginning of my employment. The confusion turned out to have been nothing more than a clerical error, but the correct amount felt a fortune. I was delighted and when I wrote to my father he was also very pleased. Salaries in engineering are normally high, but I was particularly happy because I had been comparing it to my £60 a month from my father. Jim's intervention was a blessing.

As for Freddie Laker, while he may not have been popular with a swathe of aeronautical engineers at that time, with me he was always very pleasant. Each time he saw me he asked how I was, going out of his way to say, "Hello Nazie, how are you doing?"

I saw him a couple of times on the planes. He used to sit up front in first class, and I always made sure that the seat next to him was not occupied because he once told me he liked the space as it enabled him to work without distraction.

In the years that followed, I even ended up being his unofficial personal chauffeur.

This all started when he asked me to drive him home in my navy blue Mustang. But it turned out that our destination wasn't his own home. Instead, he used to ask me to take him to his girlfriend's house in Crawley, a few miles from Gatwick and six miles from my new home in Haroldsea Drive, Horley, Surrey.

I had managed to obtain a mortgage to buy this semi-detached cottage with three bedrooms. And now, here I was, driving around one of the most influential men in aviation in my Mustang – it was my baby, and very impressive.

Our destination was kept a secret between us for a long while and, because Laker trusted me, whenever he wanted a lift somewhere he would ask me to take him. He had an official driver, but I didn't even tell my friends about our secret journeys.

And naturally, Freddie loved the Mustang.

He may have been my rich and successful boss but I always felt very relaxed with him; We were both very ambitious and he was a very pleasant guy to talk to. We talked about company politics, staff shortages and operations while we were driving. "Are there things we can improve?" he would enquire. "Send me a memorandum about it." He was always asking for memoranda, and I used to send him quite a few.

The upshot of one of them was that he improved the boarding process so that the passengers weren't left standing around like chickens in a cage at the gate while we finished our pre-flight engineering checks, but were able to stay seated there until the aircraft was ready. He was always very hands-on and would discuss details with anyone working for him. And most of the time, he listened.

He even wanted to find out what the handlers needed. These are the guys who put the chocks under the wheels when an aircraft arrives at the stand and who make sure the fire extinguishers are in position. He made the time to listen, which was something I admired him for.

Freddie made BUA profitable, but by 1967 had quit to pursue his dream of starting his own airline. A very clever businessman, he went on to become the inventor of low-cost air travel and a real pillar of the aviation industry; certainly a man to admire. No-one thought Laker Airways would last but its no frills, cut-price route across the Atlantic – known as Skytrain – was a success, securing Laker's reputation as the pioneer who paved the way for all the other cut-price carriers, such as Virgin, Ryanair and Easyjet, to follow. Freddie Laker was knighted in 1978 in recognition of his services to the airline industry

Before he left BUA he barnstormed one of his new VC10s across Latin America to show off his new routes, with none other than the Duke of Edinburgh among his passengers. This meant that the aircraft, with its four engines at the back, had to be spick and span, with everything top notch.

However, the flight very nearly didn't happen.

I was on the night shift a few hours before Prince Philip was due to depart. We were busy in our offices on the ramp, where the passengers board the planes. Line guys like me always wore a uniform because we were in contact with the customers. If there was a snag on the aircraft – an issue that needs sorting out – we would board and fix it, and that meant wearing a jacket and tie. Only the fitters and the technicians in the hangars wore overalls.

This was a job that could make the adrenalin flow, especially if there was a major fault and the plane was full of worried passengers gripping their armrests. You would see their faces and know you were there to solve the problem. It was terrifically challenging. But it wasn't always like that.

That night the boys in the hangar, a long taxiway across the runway, didn't have much to do so Arnold asked them to spruce up the plane ready for the following morning's high-profile departure.

As the supervisor that day, this was my cue. "Tow the aircraft to the hangar and give it to the technicians," I instructed.

My job was very interesting. I loved being in charge of a team that specialised in trouble-shooting defects that the plane came in with. It was a job that always gave me a challenge. Generally, the men under my control were very reliable and some of them had a lot more experience than me. But not everything always went according to plan.

Bill Boltwood was the shift leader at the hangar that day. He decided to get the mechanics to smarten the aircraft up with fresh tyres. This required each side of the plane to be jacked up separately, enabling the wheels to be removed.

His hangar mechanics had been working on the plane for a while when we heard a horrendous screeching sound coming from the hangar, followed by the deep thump of imploding metal.

"What the fuck was that?" I shouted. As I jumped to my feet the shift leader came rushing into the office, "Go quick!" he urged me, looking distraught. Normally you always use the perimeter road, but I jumped in the Ford Escort we used and hurtled across the brightly-lit runway.

I couldn't believe my eyes.

Everybody knows that when you jack up a plane on the wings you also need a tail jack to keep it steady.

This is doubly important with a VC10 because the centre of gravity is way back, due to the presence of the four rear engines. Normally, jacking aircraft is a specialist job but the quality control inspectors who oversee this sort of thing only worked during daytime. Unwisely, Bill had taken matters into his own hands and instead of jacking each side separately he had attempted to jack the entire aircraft in order to save time and change all ten wheels simultaneously.

When I arrived in the hangar, the scene that greeted me was an appalling sight. Bill had forgotten to engage the tail jack. The screeching sound we had heard was the plane falling off the wing jacks at it tipped backwards. The thump that followed was the unused jack piercing the tail of the fuselage as it fell, pulled down by the immense weight of the engines.

There was no way that anyone, royalty or not, would be travelling in that plane for months.

We needed a solution. This was a high-profile flight which would garner a lot of publicity.

The only possible way out of this was to quickly turn around the VC10's sister aircraft.

India Whisky, as it was called, was due to arrive

back at Gatwick at 7am from a night flight. My shift was due to end then, but all of us stayed on. Teamwork at BUA and later British Caledonian, as it was to become, was always fantastic.

As soon as India Whisky arrived, I spoke to the captain and the flight engineer and we went through the tech log of defects that pilots keep during a flight so they can be rectified during the plane's brief turnaround. "Listen, we have to turn this around fast. Are any of these snags detrimental?" I urged.

We started scanning through the snags. Some are urgent. Others can wait. Line boys like me were selected to know the difference as well as for our ability to act fast and rectify defects in a very short time. With airlines, efficiency is everything.

"Okay, we can leave that one, and that one," said the captain, as he ran his finger down the list. Some of them were A snags, but he helped us by downgrading a couple of less serious issues and making them into B snags so we could get the plane ready in time.

"Windscreen heat," he said, "We'll take that off". All the cockpit windows are heated to stop ice forming, but a couple of them weren't working.

Looking pointedly at Bill Boltwood, who looked pretty embarrassed, I said, "We'll only change wheels that are bald. We will not change wheels just because of Prince Philip."

Normally it would have taken us four or five hours to turn the aircraft around after a long-haul absence, but we did it in two-and-a-quarter hours. By the time the plane was ready, I'd worked a sixteen-hour shift and was exhausted.

Believe it or not, a few days later we got a letter from the secretary of Prince Philip himself, thanking us for the extra effort we had taken to get the plane ready. He had been told about the plane falling off the jacks and how the engineers had done a marvellous job turning the other plane around so quickly. We pinned his words of gratitude to the wall of the office.

The upshot of all this was that all the engineers had to have revision courses on how to jack VC10s and Bill Boltwood got promoted to planning, a desk job that got him out of the way. It was four weeks before that aircraft was ready to fly again.

On one occasion in the late 1960s, we had important passengers of a rather different kind arriving at Gatwick.

A BCal VC10 had just arrived from Kampala, Uganda, and I was getting ready to take charge of turning it around for another service. I could see the loaders making their way towards the plane to empty the hold and deal with the cargo in the usual fashion. Suddenly, I saw the loaders flying out of the rear hold like corks out of a pop gun. They were shouting and causing a tremendous ruckus. "Chimpanzees on the loose," shouted one of them as I approached.

Indeed, there were three dozen chimpanzees running riot inside the cargo hold of the aircraft. Somehow they had managed to open the doors on their cages and get free.

Thank God they did so because their actions were destined to change the course of their lives – this live cargo had been destined for laboratory tests.

Staying very calm, I ran up to the cargo door and inched it open. A pair of startled eyes stared back at me. In the background I could see chimpanzees swinging from their crates and jumping off packing boxes. It was like a jungle gym in there.

We all had to think on our feet.

Over the next ten minutes we got hold of a variety of vehicles. Our Ford Escort van was backed up to the cargo door ready to receive the first few chimps. We also got all the fruit from the plane, including the bananas from first class.

We threw them inside the Escort, opened the cargo door and a few of the chimps went in after the fruit and started munching on it.

We did the same with the radio van and the electricians van. Soon, we were able to get some of the animals' empty cages out of the cargo bay.

"Come on, come on," I said, encouraging a few of the chimpanzees into one of the cages. I got right up close to offer the bananas, and they seemed quite placid.

We caught a lot of them, but some remained in the cargo hold. The rest of them went wild and ran all over the tarmac looking for food. We had to call the RSPCA in to round them all up.

I didn't realise the danger at the time. It was only later that I was told about the aggressive reputation of chimps when they are cornered, and discovered that they can attack if they are frightened. Apparently aggression is a common part of chimpanzee behaviour, so we were lucky that day.

And there the story might have ended if it hadn't been picked up by the newspapers. There was a public outcry about their destination which resulted in the apes being saved from the labs and sent to various zoos instead. Everybody I worked with was pleased because they were such appealing and intelligent animals, but you should have seen those loaders flying out of the hold.

Chapter Four

A LETTER FROM
MY SISTER

❧

A thousand moments that I had just taken for granted – mostly because I had assumed there would be a thousand more – Morgan Matson.

It was the most important letter I had ever written.

Writing in Arabic to please him, I proudly told my father the news that he had become a grandfather. As I slid the letter into the envelope I thought of the deep pleasure that this news would give him. Unusually, I hadn't heard from him for a few weeks and it made me happy to imagine his happiness on opening my letter.

Ferdinand Sheriff had been born by Caesarean in Crawley Hospital, in West Sussex, on 28th July 1967.

He weighed an elephantine 12lbs 13 ounces; we were told he was the heaviest new-born on record there. I have always loved children and it was a great feeling to have a child of my own.

Fernanda, my mother-in-law, came from Spain to help with the new baby. I liked to imagine the look on my father's face when he too would one day meet my wonderful boy. Unfortunately, due to the political situation in Egypt we had no idea when that would be.

My father had been due to visit me the previous month but the trip had had to be cancelled because of circumstances outside our control.

He had been very disappointed. He'd had everything ready and his letters at that time had been full of practical details that revealed, in his own unique way, how much he was looking forward to his first visit to London. He had even had new shoes made and new suits tailored especially for the visit to see me.

It had been a while; since graduation, I had thrown myself into work and London life, and latterly marriage and impending fatherhood. Being so busy, I had stopped returning home to visit my family in Egypt as often as I had while I had been a student at Chelsea College.

In fact, we had not seen each other for two years when my father had announced that he missed me very much and was going to visit me for the first time.

"What colour suits should I wear in London?" he asked me.

"A little darker than in Egypt, Ya Baba," I explained, using the Arabic phrase which translates as 'Dear Father' – there was a lot of respect towards ones' parents in those days.

"England doesn't have a lot of sunshine and people wear more sombre coloured suits than in the Middle East," I continued.

Carefully, he prepared every detail in his methodical manner, ready for his imminent trip.

But just before my father was due to leave Cairo, the Six-Day War started on 5th June 1967. False Russian intelligence claimed Israeli troops were planning to invade Syria; so Syria and its ally Egypt prepared for war. Egyptian forces were mobilised along the Israeli border but they were caught by surprise when Israel launched a pre-emptive strike on Egyptian airfields, as well as a ground offensive. In all, this led to the deaths of more than twenty-thousand soldiers from the Arab forces and rather less on the other side.

On 11th June a ceasefire was signed, but Egypt's borders remained closed and an Emergency Law was enacted, which was to remain in effect until 2012.

From our point of view, this meant that my father

was unable to visit me in London. At that time, for Egyptian nationals to leave their own country was similar to the situation in Russia. You could not just walk out of the country. You required an exit visa and none were being issued. The state of emergency extended police powers, legalised censorship and allowed the indefinite detention of civilians without trial. Free speech was also limited.

Apparently my father became very depressed by the situation. He seems to have believed that it meant it would be impossible for us to see each other again.

And then one day his letters just stopped. It was very strange.

After I had not heard from him for a few weeks I wrote to my sister, Ragaa to find out why our father was not writing to me every week or so, as he had done for the past seven years. Carmen was about to give birth to his grandson. It was an exciting time and I wanted him to be part of it.

Ragaa wrote back with the news that he was ill with diabetes. "Your father is not well. That's why he can't write to you," she explained.

I continued to write to him, waiting for a letter to arrive that would tell me he was feeling better. No letter came. "Oh, he'll be better next week," I would tell myself, busy at work and with the baby at home.

But according to Ragaa he didn't seem to be getting

any better. In fact, he was getting worse. I couldn't accept it and brushed off the news in my relentlessly positive way. Once travel restrictions were lifted and he was better I knew my father would come and see us.

I continued to keep him up to date with what was happening. They weren't long letters, but they were in Arabic; I wanted him to know I was thinking of him and could not wait for him to meet his grandson.

Another month passed. It was now six weeks since Ferdinand had been born, and still no word from my father. On leaving Cairo I had promised I would write to him every week, and at last, seven years after making my pledge, I was fulfilling my end of the bargain.

In mid-September, I received a letter from Egypt; but it was another letter from Ragaa, not from my father.

I opened the letter up, eager for news. The letter was devastating.

My father had died at the age of sixty-two.

He had gone into a diabetic coma, due to his diabetes, and this had led to "complications" including heart failure – the precise details were not revealed to me.

But worse was to come.

Reading on, the letter informed me that my father had actually died on 11th July, seventeen days before Ferdinand was born.

I had been writing to my father for two months without knowing that he had passed away.

It felt like treachery. Had I known he had died on the 11th I would have been home in Cairo by the 12th.

Instead, I had been denied the chance to pay my respects to him – in the Middle East, they bury their dead within twenty-four hours.

The brutal truth is that my father had already been dead and buried for nearly ten weeks. He had been dead when Ferdinand was born.

I took the news very, very hard.

I was furious and I was distraught. It was the worst pain I had experienced.

At a later point, after the pain of loss and the feelings of deception had subsided enough to confront my family about their decision, I asked my mother why they had not told me about his death as soon as it happened.

She explained that it was her belief that had I been told earlier I would have dropped everything and come back to Egypt permanently. She had felt strongly that this would not have been the best thing for me.

She had discussed her point of view with my brother, my sister and my two uncles. They all agreed; had I been told, they believed I would have given up my life in the UK, and returned to look after them by managing my father's estate.

She understood that fundamentally I am impulsive. By not telling me until September they believed there was less chance for spontaneity. They believed that once my son was born the urgency to return to Egypt would diminish. In hindsight, with the benefit of half a century to reflect on this, I believe they were right; I think probably that I would have dropped my life and jumped on the first aircraft home.

They had my best interests at heart but it still hurt like hell. And it still does.

After all these years, I can't shake the belief that my father died of a broken heart; that he was left deeply distraught at the idea of being unable to travel to the UK.

The Six-Day War had many victims. In some ways, I think he was one of them.

As for me, my father's death changed everything. I will never know what would have happened had he not died but I think it is likely I would have returned to Egypt after a few years.

Although happy that I came to England to study, I believe that he would have wanted me to return to Egypt in due course and to find a job with Egypt Air or United Arab Airlines, so he could see me more often.

Perhaps in years to come he would have asked me again to run the estate in Upper Egypt. And I am sure

I would have done so. My brother Nabil had trained as a doctor, and in time would become eminent, but he was a lousy businessman.

In the end, a cousin took over the land and made a success of it.

After my father died I realised that there was no longer any point in seeing my future in Egypt. I had my son and my whole conception of life had changed.

Fortunately, I was lucky because I had a job I enjoyed. My father always used to say, "You have to enjoy what you're doing at work because you will spend a third of your life doing it and if you don't enjoy it, you are killing yourself. So enjoy it, because it is something that's going to be with you a long time."

Perhaps it was 'the will of God' that I stayed in the UK, although I prefer to think of it as fate and destiny, which are in everybody's religion.

We are all shaped by our losses and my father is always on my mind. I don't idolise him and it's not something spiritual, but anything I do, he's always there, like a sixth sense; I can't really explain it, yet in every situation I face I constantly refer to him for his advice and his instructions. For me, that is his ongoing legacy and, God knows, I have needed his counsel at times – as you will see.

Chapter Five

EXPATRIATION

❧

Rule No. 1; Never lose money. Rule No.2;
Never forget rule No. 1 – Warren Buffett

Always trade in something you know about. Believe me, I learned the hard way. And it was only after a number of false starts and disastrous experiences that I got involved with aircraft parts and made my fortune.

But there were a lot of wrong turns along the way.

Since the birth of Ferdy, Carmen hadn't been working. She used to work for a small business making early computer circuit boards and had done well at this, but gave it up to look after our son.

It was then that I thought I'd better start working a bit harder, and finding ways to save money – such as my regular visits to Smithfield market to buy meat at wholesale prices, because although Carmen had given up her job she had not given up her taste for nice clothes.

I soon discovered that she owed money to a fashion boutique in Horley, and at Buncles the fishmongers where she had been buying fish on credit in order to fund the purchase of the dresses.

Discovering I had a knack for making money was fun but it was also a necessity when someone is spending 120 per cent of your income.

And at the beginning of 1967 something had happened which opened up the chance for me to think beyond my monthly pay cheque; the bosses at BUA decided to change our work pattern.

Instead of working seven days on and three days off, they changed the rota to four on, four off. Working a longer twelve-hour shift meant we would see the same aircraft departing and returning within the same shift.

Management thought it was a more productive way to use us line engineers. But it was a killer. We moved constantly from one aircraft to another. It was twelve solid hours of trouble-shooting and repair. The four night shifts from 7pm to 7am were the worst. After the fourth night shift we found we needed a whole twenty-four hours in bed to recover physically and mentally –

it's demanding, highly responsible work with no margin for error.

However, the best part of the new scheme was the four days off we were given after every set of four shifts.

This meant I had plenty of time with my family. I also started dabbling in business with friends, buying and selling motorcars.

I found I had a taste for this and I began to keep my eyes open for ways to earn a bit of extra cash.

I've always had an eye for an opportunity. The frustration at that time was that I had limited capital and was not always able to invest as I would have wished.

One such example is the mountainside that could have been mine.

Today, San Antonio is a lively resort set in a beautiful open bay on the west side of the Mediterranean island of Ibiza. It has beautiful beaches, a buzzing atmosphere and countless bars, restaurants and riotous nightclubs.

But in the late 1960s, when Carmen and I visited her sister Morag in San Antonio, Ibiza was still a largely undeveloped island that had only opened to international tourism in the late 1950s.

We arrived at the height of the island's pre-nightclub, hippy heyday. This was a time when there was nude bathing on the beach and drug taking everywhere. Carmen's sister was involved in that scene, but I wasn't interested. What did appeal was the earnest conversation Carmen was having in a bar-restaurant with a Catalan businessman which involved a lot of pointing at the mountain behind the town.

"What is he saying?" I asked.

"He says he wants to sell his land on the mountain. And he wants to know if my boyfriend wants to buy the whole site," Carmen added, laughing.

"How much does he want?" I asked, intrigued. There was clear potential for development, anyone could see that.

"He says £325," Carmen explained with a shrug.

I was kicking myself. I was only earning £175 a month. There was no way I could afford to tie up the money in a patch of stony ground I couldn't afford to develop until later.

I wish things had been different. That mountain is now the forest-clad setting for a glittering array of luxury mountainside villas with private pools and views of the Med.

And this wasn't the only golden opportunity I missed.

In the late 1960s, if you wanted to water your garden your only option was to use a jubilee clip – a small, adjustable metal ring – to attach your hosepipe to your outside tap. As a keen amateur gardener I knew from first-hand experience that this was a perfectly adequate system. Then one day in the pub I got talking to a German guy who asked if I wanted to buy shares in his new invention. He explained that it was a quick-release 'click' fitting that allowed you to unclip a hose instantly from any tap to which it was fitted.

"They are five cents a share and you have to buy 5,000 of them, but this is going to grow," he explained.

I'd never been a gambling person after my early experiences at the roulette table, and that's what this felt like; I just couldn't see the potential of his bright orange plastic connector.

"No thanks," I said. "What am I going to do with those shares? I mean anyone can use a jubilee clip."

Famous last words. The Original Gardena System was launched in 1968 and became a timeless classic. Today, Gardena is a multi-billion-dollar business; the leading brand for high quality garden tools in Europe and represented in more than eighty countries around the world. So that was another missed moment.

But it was only a matter of time before I found the right business venture.

I've always been a very sociable person, I'm an extrovert and I love company. I liked to go to the pub at that point in my life and I met a lot of people from different professions there. We enjoyed ourselves and I got to know them personally and made a lot of contacts. Many have stayed friends, and some are still in the aviation business after all these years.

A particular favourite spot of mine was the Aero Club, in Charlwood, Surrey – not far from my home in Horley. This was an exclusive club that was popular with pilots, senior engineers and flight attendants. I would head there for a few drinks with friends before going home, as did lots of pilots who would pop in for a drink after flying in to Gatwick.

It's a good thing my father had banned me from flying. Flying used to lead inevitably to the sauce, because it's a very stressful job. In those days, pilots could be on layover away from base for a long time with nothing to do. So there was an incentive to party. And believe me, pilots know how to party.

Fortunately, the Aero Club was a place where anybody could walk in after work in their uniform without causing a stir, however many stripes you had on your shoulder. And however bad your behaviour.

But not everyone I met was involved directly in aviation.

My friend David Bryantson was a luxury car dealer. One day he told me he needed an office and did I know anyone with office space to spare. I told him I did and that I would willingly take half the office space for my new venture; an air taxi business.

I had been dreaming of a fleet of executive jets, ferrying private passengers around the UK. Of course, I didn't have the money for such an ambitious project, which was an unknown business model at the time but fairly commonplace today, so I decided to start my business using a more affordable sort of vehicle.

Airline travel was beginning to expand to a wider population but getting a local taxi to the airport was still difficult because this was before the era of minicabs. Clearly, there was potential here.

I used my income from the overtime I'd taken on to rent office space from David, and soon I was able to scrape the money together to lease fairly luxurious cars, such as the Ford Zodiac and Ford Zephyr, from him as well.

I paid as I went along. The idea was that a client or perhaps a hotel would ring for a car. Generally, they would want to be taken to the airport.

With the way the new shift pattern worked, I was able to employ the professional drivers who tow aircraft – very good, cautious drivers – on their days off. Soon I had five cars and sixteen part-time drivers who were all willing to earn a few extra pounds.

This was my first ever company and it was called Auto Line. Business flourished. In time, we even got a few contracts from the airlines to move crew from one airfield to another. My best regular contract was with British Island Airways (BIA) who used to fly to Jersey and Guernsey, and had the contract to deliver the daily newspapers to the Channel Islands.

The BIA flight crew were based at Gatwick and needed transportation to Southampton and back. Although it was a four-hour round trip my drivers were happy to do it and Auto Line became very profitable.

Within two or three years, business was booming and I had seven cars running all over the place. Word had spread and we were now offering crew runs to drive a captain and first officer in style from Gatwick to London Airport (which became Heathrow Airport in 1966).

Most crew were delighted to travel in comfort in a private car instead of a large crew bus.

And there had been other developments.

In the spring of 1970 Carmen informed me, to my delight, that at Christmas I would become a Daddy for the second time; and in November I suddenly found myself working for a new airline.

The British Government's Edwards Committee had been formed in 1967 to look at the future of British aviation. Its report, published in May 1969, made a number of recommendations. One of them was that a 'second force' airline should be formed from Britain's independent operators to expand the UK's airline capacity on both short-haul and long-haul routes.

The upshot was that the Scottish charter airline Caledonian Airways took over British United Airways (BUA), then the largest British independent airline and my employer. BUA, it turned out, had financial troubles.

The result was the creation of a new company, British Caledonian Airways or BCal.

Overnight, I had found myself working for BCal rather than BUA. But fortunately nothing changed for us; I was still part of the same old engineering team, headed up by Arnold.

Less than a month after this, on 1st December 1970, I became a father for the second time, with the birth of Samantha Alice El Masry in Crawley Hospital. It was a great day. I was a very proud father and happy to have completed my family.

I was busy at work, busy at home, and busy with Auto Line.

As time went on and the business grew I had a few offers for Auto Line, but I wasn't interested in selling.

Then one morning my life changed direction radically. As soon as I started my shift, Arnold called me into his office. He had a lot of time for me and I knew I was popular on the ramp, so I wondered what this was about.

He praised my technical skill and my ability to get on with my colleagues, and then told me bluntly that I was needed abroad. The fact I spoke four languages, including Arabic, apparently made me the ideal man for the job – as did my Egyptian passport.

This last point was particularly important because it turned out that I was being sent immediately to Libya.

In January 1970, Colonel Muammar Gaddafi had taken direct control of Libya following the bloodless coup that had brought an end to the monarchy under King Idris. And in the summer of 1971, the British Government decided to give BOAC's North African routes to BCal.

Scheduled services from Gatwick to Tripoli were to be launched almost overnight, in airline terms, with BCal replacing BOAC as the designated flag carrier as part of the Government's drive to expand the UK's airline capacity. BOAC moved out and BCal moved in, ready to offer flights for the many British expats living in Libya, among others.

Arnold's decision was astute because he knew I spoke Arabic and could be "sociable with the natives", as he put it. I have my father to thank for that, with his insistence on me always writing to him in Arabic. Being an Egyptian national also made it easier for me to obtain an entry visa to Libya, as well as a work permit.

Libya and Egypt were allies. Egypt's president Gamal Abdel Nasser had been a great influence on Gaddafi and ties between the countries were strong, which meant being an Egyptian in Tripoli was destined to be a pleasant experience.

I was very much the right person in the right place at the right time.

But Arnold had another, more personal reason underlying his decision to expatriate me. He knew I was running a successful and flourishing business on the side and he wanted me to devote my energies to British Caledonian, not Auto Line. This was another motive for him sending me abroad. He was a clever man. Most pilots have side businesses but mine was very successful – Arnold didn't want to lose a good engineer, so he made me an expat instead.

Airlines are always short of engineers. Any engineer with the right qualifications is ensured of a job because the training is long and tedious. You have to get a degree and then you have to get a Civil Aviation licence. It's quite a task, which is why not many people are attracted to it. But although the job carries enormous responsibility, if you can cope with that intensity the rewards can be great because of the abundant free time that is part and parcel of the job.

I had to leave for Tripoli almost immediately which did not thrill my new wife who was left to look after Ferdy, who was nearly four, and his six-month-old baby sister, Samantha, by herself, but we made plans for Carmen and the children to join me once I was settled in North Africa. I was looking forward to settling with my young family in Libya.

But first I had to tie up a rather unfortunate loose end.

During my time at Gatwick I had sometimes had to travel to repair aircraft that had become unserviceable abroad. During these travels I had had a bit of fling with Agnes D, one of the Dutch ground staff in Amsterdam whom I saw every six months or so.

Before I went to Libya, I went back to Amsterdam with a couple of pilot friends to see Agnes for a final time to explain that I had reformed. I was, I told her, going to be a devoted father and husband, and would not be coming back. Let's just say, it wasn't an enjoyable trip. There was drama and there was crying.

I was sure she would get over it, but I was to find out in due course that I was wrong.

The other loose end was Auto Line. Naturally, being expatriated ruined my business. To my great regret, I sold it to a chap who had a taxi company in Redhill and was dying to get into the lucrative airport business.

When I look back now, I can see that devoting my attention to aviation has turned out well in my favour and that Arnold did me a huge service.

I was about to find myself away from base, in charge of a team, and with more free time on my hands than ever, with my life lived on standby. I seized what was on offer with great enthusiasm – as I did my freedom from base.

"Do what you like, provided you don't get into trouble with the locals, lad," were Arnold Sheead's parting words to me.

I would discover soon that as long as I kept a close eye on the movements of the aircraft, and knew when they were arriving so we could turn them around and get rid of them as quickly as possible, that I could be very efficient indeed with my time. This was to prove the perfect opportunity for a fledgling entrepreneur like me, as well as provide a lot of fun.

Chapter Six

A CUP OF WHISKY

⤬

*The difference between who you are and who
you want to be, is what you do – Bill Phillips*

I arrived at Tripoli Idris International Airport, as it
was then, on 1st June 1971 on the last BOAC flight
from Gatwick to Libya, with two members of British
Caledonian's senior management team. As we flew
over Libya, I was mesmerised by my first sight of the
desert below me.

When I'd left North Africa a decade earlier, I'd been
a skinny seventeen-year-old in a camel hair coat with
£60 in my pocket.

Now I was back in North Africa for the first time in
seven years as the twenty-eight-year-old head of

BCal's aeronautical engineering operations in North Africa, and a father of two.

Before we left Gatwick I was assured that all the flight spares and equipment, together with my luggage for an extended stay, would be shipped on the inaugural British Caledonian flight from Gatwick to Tripoli which would be departing, amid some fanfare, a couple of days later.

I thought no more of it as we landed in Tripoli at the small white-painted airport which was shimmering in the late afternoon heat, and took my overnight bag down the steps of the plane.

Although it has now been replaced by the ultramodern Tripoli International Airport, back then the airport still looked like the former RAF base that it had been during the war. At that time, it had served a crucial function as a staging post servicing the strategic air corridor to East Africa and the Far East. Known during the war years as Castel Idris, it is said that the transit quarters had once been the Italian officers' brothel.

I arrived two years after the RAF had departed. The searing heat of a southern Mediterranean summer's evening was reminiscent of my childhood in Cairo, 1300 miles along the coast to the east.

The airport was still like something out of

Casablanca with slow swirling fans in the ceiling, and staff wearing fezzes. A terrace outside afforded fine views of the aircraft being refuelled.

In 1957, a Hastings was said to have collided with a camel one dark night as it was crossing the runway at Castel Idris on a traditional path that predated the building of the airfield. The result? A lot of camel mince and a double propeller change.

After being escorted through immigration, the handover from the BOAC Engineering manager was brief and to the point. I met the new team I had inherited from him – two engineers, a driver and a handyman – and was told by the head mechanic that I had been invited by the airport commandant to have lunch with him and his senior staff in the old officers' mess.

I tried to explain that we could do this some other time, there was a lot to organise, after all, but he insisted. Following Arnold's instruction to be "sociable with the natives" I was delighted to accept, but it was a terrible experience.

Lunch was served on a large round table about two feet from the ground. In the centre, was a big mountain of rice with some sort of red sauce at the very top, embedded with large chunks of meat.

The senior men sat down and I was ushered to sit next to the big chief on rugs on the floor. There were no chairs so I knelt on my knees. That wasn't very comfortable so I tried crossing my legs for a bit. Once I was settled I noticed that there was no conventional cutlery either.

I looked around at my fellow diners. They were eating the rice with wooden spoons, but I found it tricky cutting up big chunks of meat embedded in rice with a spoon. They began deftly using the fingers of their right hands to extract the meat from the bones. I tried to do the same but my piece kept slipping from my fingers.

Suddenly the chief saw me struggling and reached over to my plate to help me. He clutched the bony piece of meat in his fist to trap the bones and pulled hard. Out slid an instantaneously deboned piece of meat. I was too surprised not to eat it.

The meat was rather tough and very difficult to chew.

By way of conversation, I praised them in Arabic for preparing such a feast and finished with the words, "And what sort of meat is this?"

The commandant looked very proud. "Camel meat," he declared. His manner made it clear it was a local delicacy, akin to serving lobster or caviar in Britain.

I nearly choked.

I was to discover that camel is a popular dish prized for celebrations in Libya. The ancient Persians used to serve whole roast camel at banquets, and camel meat in couscous was to become one of Colonel Gaddafi's favourite meals.

But at the time I was shocked. I didn't like it at all and soon made my excuses, explaining I had been travelling all morning and would like to go to my hotel.

From then on I was careful to avoid any menu offering camel.

I arrived at my hotel, the Al Waddan, the oldest and grandest in the country and once known as the "Waldorf Astoria of Tripoli", where I met the BCal management and relaxed with a cocktail on the terrace overlooking the Mediterranean.

Two days later we met the inaugural flight of British Caledonian from Tripoli to Gatwick.

It was a big event. There were press, chief pilots, more top management and the impending arrival of my luggage – or so I thought. After a bit of a party the Vickers VC10 was refuelled and ready for departure.

Unfortunately, starting the engines was not very successful. I went up to the cockpit and managed to start three of them, but number four just would not light up. I was confident that this could be sorted out easily. I instructed my engineers to fetch the necessary tools to change one of the igniter plugs, a straightforward enough task.

But there was a problem. The engineers could not find any of the necessary tools or spares on board. We contacted London who assured us that everything was in the rear hold.

The engineers looked. It was empty; no tools, no spares. And of course, there had been no luggage. It turned out that the load control officer had had to lose some weight from the aircraft. To 'trim it' to the right weight, he'd removed the tools, the spares and my suitcases.

The lack of spares meant that the aircraft could not carry passengers and the inaugural flight from Tripoli to Gatwick ended up being nothing more than a ferry flight; a fact that BCal managed to keep out of the newspapers the following day.

The lack of luggage meant I was once again living out of the single small suitcase I had brought with me.

To my delight, following this incident I became very popular with top management and they started to include me in all their functions and activities.

I stayed at the Al Waddan for more than six weeks in all and had a ball while a large villa was being redecorated and furnished ready for the arrival of my family in time for Christmas 1971.

It had been the home of a British Airways engineer who was leaving the country and who showed me around. Apparently someone had told him I was Egyptian, and as he walked me around the house he explained everything to me very slowly as if I was just learning to speak English.

"This...is...the...boiler...that...heats...hot water... for...the...showers," he said slowly and clearly.

I nodded attentively, as if I was carefully processing everything he was saying. He had made an assumption that I had just arrived from Cairo. I decided to have fun with this and not say a word myself.

He led me outside. "And...this...door...leads...to... the...garage." I nodded again. This went on for a while until he said something about my wife and I said, "Oh, you mean the trouble and strife?"

He nearly fell down the stairs. "What, you speak English?" he spluttered, amazed and a bit embarrassed.

"Of course I do, and watch out for those apples and pears," I continued.

"What's this, you speak Cockney as well?" he said, thoroughly confused by now.

When the area manager told him my background we all had a laugh, but you know, people do generally underestimate what the other party can do. A lot of people can do things that you never expect them to.

Being in charge of North Africa was quite a comfortable and easy job compared to the line work I was used to and I started to really enjoy myself. Even after British Caledonian took on the handling of KLM with their DC8s it was still a doddle and left me with a lot of time on my hands.

Life under Gaddafi's new regime was quite pleasant. The country was disciplined and he respected the many expatriates working there in the oil and aviation industries. There was order and control twenty-four hours a day. He was popular when he took over, with no sign of the tyrant who would later emerge, and he was particularly popular with the foreigners whom he left alone as he needed them for the oil and the infrastructure.

To me, very green because I hadn't left Europe since I'd arrived from Egypt, Libya felt like the land of opportunity. I had plenty of money from my salary and allowances, and plenty of free time. Eventually I would tire of life in North Africa, for various reasons, but to begin with I met a lot of very interesting people and made many friends.

I even started to adapt to the Libyan way of life. I'd always had a very sensitive palate and had never been able to eat anything spicy; even white pepper was too much for me. However, after a few months I started eating spicy food. Harissa was nothing, even very spicy hot fish was a delight.

But the real excitement was the booze.

For a supposedly dry state with a prohibition on alcohol, there must have been more alcohol in Tripoli than any other major city anywhere – but all of it underground. I was able to make a life out of finding ways of supplying it.

Everywhere I go, I start planning things. How am I going to live here? How am I going to do this? And when it came to Libya the issue was the booze.

Everyone wanted it. But there were no off-licences and no airport duty free. However, the planes were full of the stuff.

My grand contraband whisky scheme all started the moment that a lovely chief hostess named Rosemary Johnson poured me my first Glenfiddich whisky in a tea cup and saucer after her plane touched down. From then on, she always used to put it in the front toilet in first class and would smile and say to me, "Nazie, your tea is getting cold". I would sip my little Glenfiddich 'tea' while signing the tech log, right next to the customs guy standing next to me – the idiot – and soon I was really singing.

That was in my earliest days in Libya, but it gave me an idea. Soon I had refined the plan and developed a way of getting contraband booze in, right past the noses of the customs officers.

It was, if I say so myself, a brilliant scheme.

I travelled home every couple of weeks for a night or two to see Carmen and the children. They were quick trips and while I was away my boys, two young mechanics, used to cover me. If I wanted to go a bit longer I used to ask for an engineer to replace me for a week or so. It was lovely to see my family, but there was a secondary reason for leaving Libya.

On the way back through Gatwick I would hit the duty free and buy a bottle of Scotch, a bottle of gin, a bottle of Vodka and maybe two bottles of Scotch – it all depended what everyone wanted.

And, before I left Horley, I also used to pop into the local Tesco to buy vacuum packs of Wall's bacon. All the expats in Tripoli loved bacon so there was nothing out of the ordinary about this.

I would put the bottles in my suitcase under my clothes, and then I would put the packs of bacon strips on top of the clothes.

When I went through customs I used to call out, "Who's going to clear my luggage?" I would then open the suitcase and say loudly, "Lahm el Khanzeer, Lahm el Khanzeer" – which means 'pork meat' in Arabic.

Something in the ancient Libyan brain does not like pork at all because pork is of course banned in most Islamic countries, along with alcohol.

"Eurgh, close it quickly," they would cry out in Arabic.

"Are you sure?" I would ask.

"Yes, close it, off you go."

It was so easy. I had more whisky than the Highlands.

Friday was our day off and every week we went to someone's house. Then all the booze would come out and we would have a ball. I never made any profit, in fact it was a dead loss. But we were not in it for the money. Expats had a generous salary and enough allowances to keep us living in comfort – a state of affairs nicely lubricated by my amateur liquor import business.

Interestingly, the Libyan customs officers got wise eventually to what I was doing and I used to supply contraband to half of them too.

In Libya, it's all about who you know.

Before his death, my father used to know the Egyptian ambassador to Libya and one day the ambassador, whose name was Fakhre El Dien, invited me to his house in Tripoli.

It was a slightly surreal encounter because Anwar Sadat was also there. I shook hands with the new president of Egypt in the drawing room, which contained elegant contemporary furniture and Aubusson tapestry chairs, reminiscent of the ones we'd had at home in Egypt.

What struck me most about Sadat as he greeted me with a warm handshake was that his palm felt so very silky.

The ambassador explained who I was.

"Mr Nazie works for the airline," said El Dien.

"EgyptAir?" asked Mr Sadat.

"No, sorry, I work for a British airline," I told him.

"Oh my wife Jehan is half British, her mother is English," said Mr Sadat, who had taken office the previous year.

Indeed, Jehan Sadat is the daughter of an Egyptian surgeon father and an English music teacher mother, Gladys Cotterill, whose father had been a Sheffield City police superintendent. Mrs Sadat had been born in Egypt and raised as a Muslim, according to her father's wishes, but she also attended a secondary Christian school for girls in Cairo, like me.

The president and I hit it off really well and Fakhre El Dien asked me to stay for lunch at his very long dining room table. There were only five of us and we occupied just the northern end.

Conversation flowed easily in Arabic, again I had my father to thank for that. And as we talked we ate sautéed lamb, spicy oven-baked fish and vegetables simmered in tomatoes. There was not a drop of booze on offer.

Mr Sadat struck me as a true gentleman; he was very self-deprecating. The funniest thing is that we both discovered we liked to eat salad with a very English dressing of vinegar, olive oil and lemon juice.

"It's best when it's eaten the following day out of the fridge," I said. "I really like leftover salad."

"So do I!" he declared as dessert was served. This consisted of plates of chopped fruit and a big glass dish of sickly-sweet Lebanese sweets, which I avoided.

At the end of lunch we shook hands.

"I'll have to see you again," said Mr Sadat. I was happy about that. He didn't make you feel like he was a head of state, or anything. The responsibility of switching Egypt's Cold War allegiance from the Soviet Union to the United States, a project in which he was immersed at that time, was something he seemed to wear very lightly. He just made you feel comfortable.

But unfortunately the poor fellow got shot.

The ambassador and I continued to stay in touch. I always made a point of visiting him on Fridays or Saturdays. One day, I told him that I had been trying to brew my own beer, with a beer-making kit I'd brought with me from the high-street chemist Boots on a trip home to the UK. But it was always a disaster. The resulting brew always stank of yeast. I couldn't get rid of the smell.

I had mentioned this to a pilot who told me to use only half the liquid and leave the yeast to settle.

I tried but it was still no good. When I next saw the ambassador I mentioned my failed attempts to make beer so he started sending me cases of Pilsner beer, a Czech beer, which is very, very good.

In December, Carmen and the children came to join me in Tripoli at the villa and we sent Ferdy to the International School.

We lived in a modern area, popular with expats, called Georgian Poppely. I joined our local golf club, although this never involved playing any golf. The golf course was miles away; an unappealing strip of sand in the desert.

I have never forgotten the scene in the supermarket near our house; you could tell the wives of the oil engineers working in the deserts. Mostly Americans, they would spend the daytime with hair curlers on their heads waiting for their men to return from the oil fields.

But trouble was in store. While Carmen was visiting our home in England for a short break in the spring, she saw a tall, distinguished woman lingering outside the window, who then started peering inside. Carmen opened the door and asked if she could help. Agnes introduced herself and said she only wanted to see where I lived. She and Carmen started comparing notes and, in short, I was soon worse than pork in a synagogue. The slight fling turned out to be a major disaster. My wife was disappointed and started the separation process. I tried to explain that it was all over, that I had given up such activities and was going to be a good husband, but she insisted on a divorce. I was devastated. I did not know at the time that she had already lined up an alternative solution.

Fortunately, it turned out she was happy for me to have the children, so I was given custody of Ferdy and little Samantha, leaving Carmen free to remarry in due course.

My mother was very upset about my divorce. Shortly after I told her what had happened she responded in a very practical way by sending me the daughter of one of her servants in Cairo to look after the children. Her name was Soad and the children adored her. Soad could not read or write but she learned to cook and, in all, she was to stay with us for thirty-two years. It seems fitting that her name means 'happiness' in Arabic.

I carried on in charge of North Africa which, as well as Libya, involved spending time in Tunisia and in Casablanca in northern Morocco.

It was quite exciting, particularly in Casablanca where our aircraft would arrive for a stopover in the middle of the night with a whole set of crew going south and another set going north. Some of the crew used to do the South American run; the return trip could last up to twenty-one days, so you can imagine the close relationships that formed and the intimacies that were shared.

People outside the airline industry have a curiosity about what happens on these stopovers. They assume it means partying nights away in exotic locations and exploring the local nightlife. Well, in Casablanca in the 1970s that was absolutely true; this was still the era of extended rest for flight attendants and pilots.

While the other residents of the hotel were having their breakfast, we were having supper and a drink — and usually rather more than one drink. Our lives were lived in reverse, and a lot more than sleeping occurred on some of these overnights.

I'd just got divorced and was falling in love with everyone I met. I really had a hell of a good time, but thank God these encounters did not last very long. The best part with trips abroad is that there is an understanding among the crew that as soon as the plane lands back in London the communication and closeness disappears and everyone goes back to their own way of life — although there were always exceptions and some people did pair up in the real world.

As an Arabic speaker I was perfectly placed to look after the crew on their layovers in Casablanca.

After supper I would take them out to find something exciting to do in the romantic North African city, where the smell of spices in the Kasbah vied with the tang of the Atlantic breeze. There were snake charmers and night clubs and every kind of vice imaginable. It was a seriously wild place and I was happy to oil the wheels. According to one pilot, spending time there with me was "wondrous fun".

Just outside the hotel grounds was a bordello, strategically placed to cater to the foreign visitors staying there. I often used to go there for a drink with the crew which included the pilots, the engineers and one or two stewards, and most of our charming female cabin staff who always seemed intensely curious to step foot inside a real Moroccan brothel.

Our air hostesses looked very nice once they removed their uniforms and dressed in civvies. When we first started turning up for a drink there, the madam of the bordello was rather apprehensive and there was a degree of confusion.

I would arrive with different groups of young women and eventually she complained that the sight of these attractive western girls was ruining her business. I had to explain that our girls were not on the game and that although I was their colleague, I was certainly not their pimp. She was relieved to hear that there was no threat to her business and we got on very well from that point on.

My brother was building his medical career at this point and when I heard he was coming to a medical conference in Beirut, Lebanon, I jumped on a flight to see him. I was staying at the Phoenicia Hotel and he was in the Holiday Inn. We arranged to meet at a bar. When he arrived he looked around, assuming I'd be at one of the tables. It was only when he looked up at the stage that he saw his wayward younger brother; I'd been dragged up on stage by a gorgeous belly dancer and was mid-way through a riotous belly dancing routine.

Chapter Seven

WILD TIMES IN
AMSTERDAM

❧

Never hit a man when he is down. You may find he's bigger than you when he gets up – Joas Alberto Santos Silva

By the end of 1972 I was beginning to tire of North Africa. There is only so much fun you can have in a desert. I had had enough of power cuts and water shortages followed by flooded roads when it did rain – which, surprisingly, it did quite heavily in winter. I missed the clean hospitals we have in Europe as well as the clean roads. I also yearned to see green trees rather than parched shrubs and palms.

I was also losing patience with the Islamic way of life. During Ramadan, the Islamic month of fasting,

Muslims don't eat from dawn to dusk and so nothing was open before sunset. All restaurants and coffee shops were closed during the day and life came to a complete stand still. I tried telling people that Ramadan did not apply to me because I was a Christian, but nobody took me seriously. In the end, I gave up and used to eat and drink only after sunset like everyone else, but I didn't like it and was fed up with this restrictive way of life.

The place had also left me with a bad taste in my mouth. My wife had divorced me there, and when I commuted to Tunisia and Casablanca I travelled without my children, which made me unhappy.

So when Arnold offered me the chance to head up British Caledonian's aeronautical engineering operations in Amsterdam I was enthusiastic.

By now, thanks to the generous BCal travel allowances, my salary was almost as high as a captain's. It was a good income but it came with a caveat from Arnold; "Naz, lad, you can do what you like in Amsterdam as long as you keep your nose clean."

I took a large apartment near Schiphol Airport.

Einsteinlaan 73 (in Holland the house numbers always follow the street name) was on the seventh floor and had a beautiful view of the airfield. You could also see Amsterdam, laid out on the horizon, six miles to the north-east. The land in Holland is so flat you can see everything between your vantage point and the horizon by simply turning your head.

Soad set about resuming her responsibility of looking after the whole family from the domestic point of view, and I settled into work and fatherhood.

It was ironic that I had lost my marriage because of a fling conducted in Amsterdam that it was now too late to resume, but I deserved no more than that.

There was a lot of air traffic in Amsterdam, owing to the various routes we had. This meant eight planes most days, and sometimes as many as twelve. These included the Lagos flights, as well as a regular Boeing 747 stuffed full of tomatoes from Las Palmas in the Canary Islands, a place famous for its tomato plantations. The story goes that in 1885 an Englishman arrived on Gran Canaria and planted the islands' first tomato seeds. They haven't stopped growing since. The climate proved to be so well suited to tomato growing that up to 350,000 tonnes of the things are exported a year.

"Can you handle it by yourself with two mechanics?" Arnold had asked me and I assured him that I could.

Ferdy started at the International School in

Amsterdam, where English was spoken. I felt if he went to a Dutch-speaking school it would hinder his progress as he had never spoken it before – although in time he was destined to become fluent with no discernible accent in either language. Samantha, who was still an infant, was able to start her education in a Dutch school and went on to master the language well, all the way to her eventual graduation from Amsterdam University. But that was years away.

On the way home one day, I shared the lift in the apartment block with a young lady eating an apple.

"I'm trying to go on a diet," she said, smiling.

"You look healthy enough to me," I replied.

"Thank you, but I need to lose a few pounds," she insisted.

I liked her, so I invited her to meet the rest of my family and asked her to join us for supper. That was the end of Sita's diet.

Sita De Boer loved Soad's rich Egyptian home cooking and got on particularly well with Samantha, who was now a toddler. After supper Sita read her a story, and I invited her to visit us again later that week.

A few days later, after I had put the children to bed, Sita asked if I would like to have a drink at her place; number 75. I accepted with pleasure and our cosy, neighbourly romance started.

It suited me very well. After dinner I would read to the children and tuck them into bed. Then I used to go next door and spend time with Sita, who worked as a secretary for an aerospace manufacturer, until the small hours, before returning to my apartment and sleeping until the children woke me up. It was an amicable arrangement that lasted for a year or so; I was not yet ready for anything permanent, although Sita was destined to remain a close family friend until her death from a heart attack in 2016.

As the months went by, air traffic through Amsterdam became increasingly hectic, and my two engineers and I were quite busy during our night shifts. Our job was to inspect and repair the planes when needed. At times, when an aircraft was seriously defective we used to get extra assistance from London where an entire team of engineers was based; they would fly out and help carry out the repairs. This fact also made the job very sociable, which I enjoyed. The engineers as well as the crew – the pilots and the flight attendants – would stay at the airport hotel, and the fact that I lived near the airport meant I could take a full part in the after-hours fun.

I'd chosen to live in Badhoevedorp, only three miles from Schiphol, so if there was a problem – if an aircraft wouldn't start for example – I could get there quickly.

The ticket desk would call and say, "Nazie, trouble. Can you come over?" I would immediately hop in my company car and within three or four minutes I was on the tarmac. But such proximity also had social advantages, as did my Mustang which the girls loved.

I sometimes liked to go out on the town with the girls and the pilots, and we would come back in the early morning a bit the worse for wear. The pilots especially so; I don't know why they drink more than anyone else, but back then they had a bit of a reputation for it. This was probably because they had so much time on their hands and drank through sheer boredom.

I could write a book just about the way people behave when they are abroad.

One morning I got to the airport and a pilot I'd been carousing with the night before could not be found anywhere. Eventually, I went to the airport's Hilton Hotel, where we had an account, and found him in the bar, completely paralytic.

After driving him to the airport, I strapped him into the plane and did his pre-flight checks for him. The first officer then flew the plane back to Gatwick – they are generally the more coherent of the two after a night out.

On another occasion, the problem was with the flight engineer of a Boeing 707 jet airliner. The 707 is the long-range, four-engine plane which heralded the era of mass air travel, and which could also be adapted to carry freight, but, unlike modern jets, the 707 required the presence of a flight engineer in the cockpit as well as the two pilots.

On this particular evening these three integral parts of the aircraft had gone down town for the evening, and later that night I got a call at home from the captain.

"Nazie, we have a problem, can you come and meet us in the bar?"

When I reached them half an hour later the flight engineer was in a very bad way; blood was pouring out of a nasty head wound, his nose was swollen and his ears were cut.

"What the hell happened?" I asked.

It turned out that when they had left the bar the first time, the flight engineer hadn't wanted to go back to the hotel. He had wanted to go straight back downtown. Unfortunately, he had tried to get on to a moving tram that had its doors closed.

I drove him to the hospital and waited while they patched him up. The problem was that the freighter was due to depart to Lagos the following morning and, without a flight engineer in the cockpit, it wouldn't be able to fly.

We needed to find a way around this.

It was the captain who came up with the solution.

"We won't use our headsets so he doesn't have to put his earphones on; we'll communicate using the speakers on the instrument panel," he instructed.

But of course we had to hush it up. If head office had found out, the three of them would have been for the high jump.

I've always believed that you should never hit a man when he is down. I took the same approach in life with a few guys I knew who were down on their luck and owed me money; I let them go. Everyone deserves support or a second chance.

I always got on well with the pilots. They are very quick thinkers who have to remember to do many things at the same time while remaining, to a certain extent, calm.

They were generally very likeable people and they trusted me. The hierarchy between the pilot and the senior engineer can be very mutually respectful if you can make it work and so I always made it my business to always be on hand to meet our flights in person.

My friend Frank Brejcha, who was one of our co-pilots, remembers that I'd be up on the flight deck very soon after landing to enquire if the aircraft was okay from a technical point of view and what fuel was required for the return or onward flight.

He recalls that I would set up the refuelling of the

plane and then I'd also set up the refuelling of the pilots and cabin crew, asking if anyone wanted beers, before taking their orders, a fiver from each, and zipping off in my truck to get them from the crew duty free shop.

For a while, it was Stella Artois but then their tastes changed and Grolsch beer became their favoured tipple to take back to Gatwick.

"At Gatwick, everyone always knew where we had come from as the whole crew staggered off the tarmac with flights bags and cases of beer under each arm," says Frank, who was co-pilot on the BAC 1-11 from 1978 to 1984. "Even the girls were carrying their perfume purchases, or their new Ray Ban sunglasses."

Another pilot, Don Eckford, remembers the way I would encourage the Hilton to keep their pool and sauna open late, or open it early, ready for the crews' arrival. I also knew a few of the shop assistants at the airport who would give my colleagues discounts and save them paying the high airport prices. Apparently all this made me very popular indeed.

Ultimately, pilots are putting their lives in our hands, as well as the lives of their passengers. If something goes wrong with the aircraft, the buck stops with the engineering department who are responsible for keeping the plane safe.

I learned early in my career that aircraft safety always comes first, even when you are under pressure from ops (Operations) to hurry up and let the passengers board.

This was a particular problem at the start of my career when I was a junior licensed technician and we didn't have a lot of spare planes available. If an aircraft needed to be withdrawn from service, another had to take its place which created a problem for planning.

"Can we get on with boarding now?" they would say.

"No," I would reply.

"The passengers are waiting."

"I'm sorry, but no. This is dangerous. We have to find out what is wrong."

In those days, the engineer always had the last say, but you had to have tremendous confidence when you were being pressurised by the office; both to stand up to them and in your own technical decision-making. However, when it comes to flight safety, if you're not happy with something – no matter who is pressuring you – you have to say "no".

And the pilots respect you for that, of course. Because the bottom line is that the engineers are responsible for keeping them alive. And you don't mess about because there is no substitute for safety, ever.

While most pilots are fine people, there was occasionally a bad apple in the tree. Captain Les was one such character from my Gatwick days. He was the first really tricky pilot I encountered, and was always complaining. It was as if Captain Les had not simply got out of bed on the wrong side, but been born on the wrong side of it.

Things came to a bit of a head the day I was called to the cockpit to deal with a faulty valve at the end of a long shift. It was very early morning and Captain Les was preparing the aircraft for departure. At this point, together with my colleague Gordon McKenzie, I had a reputation as a bit of a whizz kid in defects.

"How can I help?" I asked brightly.

"The air conditioning valve won't open," moaned the captain.

I diagnosed the problem, fixed it with the help of my fitters, and was just about to leave the cockpit when he said laconically, "Oh, and this one's not working either."

I solved that problem and then he thought of another issue. He was really beginning to get my goat.

At this point, I was sitting in the captain's seat and he was standing up, surrounded by his cabin crew who were all girls and had come to scrutinise the source of the delay; me.

When Captain Les came up with yet another

problem, I was quite sure this time that there was no defect and told him so.

He was not convinced.

"Alright, alright, I'll tell you what to do with all your defects," I said, fuming. "Just write all the complaints in the book, go back to operations and we'll call you when we are ready."

An hour later, just as I was about to head home at the end of my shift, I was summoned by Arnold Sheead. I walked into his office, bypassing his secretaries, and sat down in front of him.

He did not look happy.

"You know lad, you can't humiliate the bloody captain in front of his women," he boomed.

It turned out that Captain Les had indeed gone back to operations; and reported me. Apparently he thought I'd said, "Fuck off back to operations".

And now it was me getting the bollocking. Arnold was always a straight-shooter who called a spade a spade with no sightseeing.

I defended myself valiantly. Normally I never swear in front of ladies and to the best of my knowledge I had not told anyone where to go that day. But faced with the spectre of Captain Les at the end of a fourteen-hour shift there was always that outside chance…

However, from that point on Captain Les's approach changed and he became much more mild-mannered. In fact, a few years later we even became friends after my children were stranded in Ibiza with their mother but needed to get back to school. The plane was full so I called ops and asked if they could help.

As it happened, the pilot that day was Captain Les. Ops suggested Ferdy and Samantha could share one of the seats used by the flight attendants, but when Captain Les heard that Nazie's children were on board he wouldn't hear of it.

Instead, he insisted that the children would travel up front in the cockpit with him, and he opened both jump seats so they would be comfortable. It was really admirable of him and I never forgot his kindness. After I thanked him for helping my family, we got to know each other better and our friendship began.

Most of the work was fairly routine, but sometimes I ended up dealing with unusual situations, such as the day three 30-litre drums of industrial glue decanted their contents inside the cargo hold of an aircraft en route from London to Amsterdam.

The drums were supposed to be kept upright, but in order to get them into the plane the loaders had turned them on to their sides and rolled them. By the time the plane arrived in Amsterdam the lids had worked their way loose and the floor of the hold was a sticky mess. It was vital that we worked fast to prevent the glue spreading any further.

Piles of sand were kept on the airport in case of fires, so I told the cleaners from the airport ground handling company to push some of it into the glue to mop it up so it could be cleaned away. We then had to do a pressure test. This is when the aircraft is pressurised to check that no damage has been caused to the integrity of the fuselage following an incident – even a glue spill.

It appeared that the sand trick had worked and I ended up being praised for handling the situation quickly and safely. I don't know why, but it even ended up in the next edition of British Caledonian's company magazine.

A few months later I got to be a pin-up, starring as Mr April in the 1987 Schiphol Airport Authority calendar. No less than fifty-thousand copies were printed as a giveaway to passengers and staff. The photographer wanted a connection with an aeroplane, so I borrowed the headset from a mechanic and stood in front of the VC111. That photo – a companion shot of which is the front cover of this book – certainly got me noticed and I made even more new friends at the airport and further afield.

Schiphol Airport was built in 1916 as a military

airfield used by the Dutch Air Force during the Second World War. It was constructed on land reclaimed from the bottom of a lake that enabled it to be flooded as a defensive line.

At that point, the military airfield was not much more than grassland with a few sheds serving as hangars for the first aircraft. The planes were made of pipes with wooden frames spanned with linen, and the first airport staff had an equally rudimentary life. They had to wash themselves with water from the Ringvaart canal and their homes were humble barracks lit by lanterns.

Apparently, the local farmers did not want to have anything to do with modern aviation and would hurl cabbages and potatoes at the airmen as they passed by.

Due to its location on reclaimed land four metres below sea level, heavy rain often transformed huge sections of the airfield into a quagmire. KLM had to hire sturdy men to carry passengers to the aircraft on their backs.

In 1937 a tarmac runway system was built – it was the first such system in Europe. From that point on, the airport just grew and grew.

But it never moved from its naturally muddy location.

During wet weather the soft ground would become waterlogged. This wasn't really a problem because the aeroplanes were supposed to stay on the tarmac.

But one day, the First Officer of a BAC 1-11 that had just landed pulled on the rudder instead of the tiller – the tiller is used to turn the nose wheel when taxiing below a certain speed. This was a silly mistake on the part of the First Officer.

With the application of the rudder, the plane shot sideways off the runway into the soft Schiphol clay. The first I heard of this was a phone call telling me that a plane was sinking into the mud. When I arrived the passengers were being evacuated through the slurry, and they were covered in it.

Our only option was to call the fire brigade and ask them to bring their high pressure airbags immediately; these are more commonly inflated in order to move or manipulate metal following a car crash, either to free a trapped car crash victim or to gain access to a part of the vehicle.

We asked the fire brigade to inflate a number of airbags under the wings, with the intention of keeping the engines out of the mud. The runway was shut down while we battled for 48 hours to salvage the aircraft. It was a hell of a job. We had to syphon the fuel tanks from the access panels on the top of the wings. This made the plane weigh less and meant we could increase the air pressure in the airbags. At this point, a couple of my colleagues wanted to light up the engines to taxi the plane out, but I was adamant.

"No way," I insisted. "These engines are worth several million apiece; no way we are going to do such a stupid thing. We'll have to tow it out."

I knew we couldn't tow using the nose leg alone, it would have sheared off due to the weight of the clay bogging down the plane. "We have to move it with all three legs together."

Once we had strapped up all three legs we hitched the aircraft up to a tractor and started the very slow process of moving the plane backwards, inch by inch.

The 1-11 is a heavy plane, it weighs 80 tonnes empty, and this process was a delicate and careful inch-by-inch extraction. As the plane gradually began to move we inserted metal plates for the wheels to roll on. Eventually we got it into the hangar for cleaning and in two days it was flying again.

There was a similar incident in 2014 at Schiphol when the nose wheel of a Boeing 747 travelling from Nairobi to Amsterdam ended up in the muddy grass next to the runway, following brake problems. No-one was hurt but it was an hour before the passengers were able to leave the jumbo jet.

Aircraft are exactly like human beings. When a schoolboy has the 'flu, you can bet your life that the dormitories are full of other schoolboys with the 'flu.

And it's the same with planes. If a valve on a plane fails, you can bank on the fact that the same valve will fail on a plane of the same age and type a few days, weeks or months later. It's amazing how defects go from one aircraft to another. Part of the job of a commercial aeronautical engineer is developing the sort of internal human hard disc that can remember all the defects that happened on a similar aircraft years ago.

Once you know the system, it's not complicated anymore. And if you can't remember a system – such as the air conditioning or the landing gear, for example – then you go back to the books or the training films, and run them chapter by chapter or frame by frame to look for the problem.

Hugh Morgan, one of the senior engineers at Gatwick, taught me always to start from scratch with the basics and begin my checks by looking for something obvious – whatever the pilots may be telling you.

"Never mind the fucking pilots, ignore them," he would insist. "All you have to do is start from the beginning."

I learned that the first step is always to go into the cockpit and check the right switches are on, just as with a domestic appliance. Usually that fixes the problem, but if it doesn't, the next step is to go direct to the source and have a look under a panel so you can see it directly for yourself.

It's all about trouble-shooting, and I always thrived on the analytical challenge of trying to work things out.

But this didn't extend to trying to land a plane I wasn't qualified to fly when the pilot disappeared mid-flight.

Fortunately, there were no passengers on this particular flight to Jersey, which made things slightly better. I had hitched a ride with two mechanics on the daily Dakota freight run to the Channel Islands, together with the islands' newspapers, in order to fix an unserviceable aircraft.

As it was a freighter configuration, the pilot let me sit next to him on the starboard side in a cockpit seat. We'd been airborne for half an hour of the seventy-minute flight when captain Jimmy had an idea.

"You've got a PPL [pilot's licence] haven't you?" he asked.

"Of course I have," I replied.

"Okay then, take the controls and continue on the same heading," he said, unclipping his seat belt.

And then he just disappeared into the back of the aircraft.

He was gone for some time.

After a while I started getting worried about the landing bit which is tricky in a DC-3.

Soon I could see the hazy outline of the islands on the horizon, and then the radio crackled into life. It was the control tower at Jersey airport.

"Jimmy, where the hell are you?" I shouted. "I can see the bloody runway!"

There was silence for a moment and then I heard footsteps.

"It's alright lad, I'm here. Don't panic," said Jimmy as he rushed back into the cockpit.

He ended up landing it, but I almost had kittens that day. It had to remain a secret or he would have lost his job, because I certainly wasn't qualified to fly a DC-3, let alone land a fully loaded one.

Working for BCal was always a really pleasant experience; it was a unique airline. We all knew each other very well and tended to work hard and play hard, with a fierce loyalty to the company and to our chairman, Sir Adam Thomson.

The air hostesses helped the engineers. The engineers helped the porters. The porters helped the handlers. It was all like one big family and you felt it. When it was cold the girls used to make tea for all the staff and when the cleaning gang came up they used to give them drinks as well. And I'd say, "Make sure you think of Jock."

"Who's Jock?" they'd ask.

"He's in charge of the honey cart today," I'd explain. That's what they call the toilet wagons, and he used to have to drain these things from under the fuselage. The girls would make him a tea and he'd be so happy.

At one point at the beginning of my career, I instigated a 'working-in-the-dirt' bonus for the fitters doing anything connected to toilets or drains. Arnold didn't like the idea much to start with but I thought it was only fair, particularly when there were fairly disgusting things to deal with which there often were.

An integral part of working for BCal at this time were the inevitable crew parties in the airport hotel, sometimes with a captain or two from the North African days.

The destination for these soirees was always either the captain's room or the room belonging to the number one; the senior hostess. We'd take a serious quantity of alcohol upstairs and the airport hotel would turn a blind eye to all the drinking that was going on.

My party trick at this time was to drive the wheels of the Mustang up on to the carpet outside the electric doors at the entrance to the Hilton. There were pressure sensors under the flooring that would open the doors and my challenge was to get the hotel doors to open with the weight of wheels alone. I managed it several times, but the next day, when sober, I'd always look at what I'd done and couldn't believe it I'd managed it.

As I got to know the city better, the pilots loved coming to Amsterdam and would call me up. A lot of them used to look forward to having a night stop in Amsterdam and a bit of fun with Nazie. I've been told by one former First Officer that I had a reputation among the pilots for being a "bubbly extrovert personality".

One place I used to take them was a strip club called the Casa Rosa. Word got out among the flight attendants and they always wanted to come too. "You have to take me to see the live show," they would plead.

The captain would nod and say, "Go on, Naz".

So we all used to go to Casa Rosa and I became a regular customer.

In fact, I went there so often even the performers got to know me. There was one guy who used to wear a Batman mask while he was 'performing' on stage. When we arrived he used to pause for a moment and call out, "Hi Sir, how are you". It really made me laugh and the airline girls thought it was hysterical.

It was during this time I got to know one of the Dutch

girls who flew for our airline; her parents also lived near the airport and we would sometimes go out together. This started after I noticed that she would always plan a work task that meant we would end up alone together, which I didn't mind at all. She was friendly, outgoing and good company. When she was in Amsterdam she would borrow dresses from my friends to go out for the night. She was a great party girl.

And she was a talker. One day I got on the plane to be greeted with the widest smiles from the flight attendants.

"Congratulations Nazie," one of them said and giggled.

This continued for a few more days. Every time I had a reason to get on the plane I would be met with smiles and, increasingly, questions. How had we met, when and where?

In the end I found out that she had announced to the girls that we were in a steady, serious relationship. Now that this had become official aircrew news I seemed suddenly to have become rather popular, but I didn't particularly want the attention because I was determined to remain single for a while yet – a fact that was proving increasingly alarming to my mother.

She came visiting that summer from Cairo with a clear agenda; she wanted to find a bride for me. She was very religious and we had several arguments on the subject of match-making. I stressed the fact that I was not yet ready for another permanent relationship. The truth was that I was having too much fun. This, however, was a fact I did not choose to share with my mother, although she was about to find out.

Commercial aviation is a job where there has always been a demand for women and from my point of view at that time in my life this was ideal; as was the fact that my senior status meant I was not stuck in the hangar, a place traditionally full of men.

At Schiphol, female operators tended to be in charge of the aviobridge – the enclosed, movable gangway which commonly extends from an airport terminal gate to an aircraft, enabling passengers to board and embark easily in all weathers without the need to climb stairs or venture on to the tarmac.

I got to know the aviobridge operators well because sometimes the bridge would not connect satisfactorily and then they needed our assistance. There was one particular girl who caught my eye. Her name was Cory M. She was pretty, a little bit cocky and very slim. We started seeing each other and even went on holiday a few times. She was very enthusiastic, in all ways, and that suited me just fine until my mother came to stay with us.

While my mother was helping with the children and

enjoying the sights of Amsterdam, I managed to get away for a few days for a short vacation with my lovely aviobridge operator, although I certainly didn't tell my mother where I was going.

Cory and I returned late from our trip and she went straight into my bedroom. I always invited her to stay in my apartment if the children were not there, and on this occasion I presumed my mother was sleeping soundly in the guest room.

In the middle of the night Cory was thirsty and went to fetch a drink of water from the kitchen. Unfortunately, my mother was not asleep, nor was she in the guest bedroom. She was, in fact, sitting on the sofa enjoying the stunning night-time view of the illuminated airport. And there was Cory, oblivious to my mother's presence in the darkened room, walking through the lounge wearing only her Victoria's Secret knickers, and no bra.

My mother was not amused. The next day she gave me a rocket about this shocking event.

"Now I know why you don't want to go out with Mona. Beauties coming in, beauties going out," she said, gathering steam. "Of course you don't want a steady relationship because you have this one here, this one there." And so it went on and on.

Mona T was a rather aristocratic Egyptian girl to whom my mother had introduced me a year or so earlier. My mother was convinced Mona was perfect for me.

Brought up in Paris, Mona had benefited from a French education. I called her the 'Vogue magazine cover' because she wore beautiful clothes, was very well-to-do, and came from a rich family who had given her a nice apartment in south-west London. Above all, my mother really approved of her.

This was odd in some ways. Mona was older than me, taller than me and smoked like a chimney, but despite all this, you could not fault her in front of my mother.

I used to travel to London to try and spend the odd weekend with Mona, but after a couple of nights I would have to make my excuses and leave her flat. We were always fine for half a day or so but then I could not bear it any longer; I had to get away from her.

The truth was, she bored me. She always said the right things, she agreed with me about everything, never argued and I had a feeling that she was trying to sink her claws into me.

I continued to try to avoid her and carried on seeing Cory and enjoying my freedom.

I also put down roots in Holland with the purchase, in 1975, of a semi-detached house in Badhoevedorp, eighteen miles from Amsterdam.

Gaaistraat 14 had a garden for the children and

with Soad's help it was turned into a happy home.

I was now fully committed to a new life in Europe. And this was significant because the previous year, in June 1974, my mother had died.

Chapter Eight

A CONVERSATION WITH MY MOTHER

༄

When you come out of the storm you won't be the same person that walked in. That's what the storm is all about – Haruki Murakami

Because Uncle Youssef was the general manager of EgyptAir in London my mother, who was one of his many distant cousins, never had any problems with her excess baggage on her return trips to Cairo after a couple of months in Europe. He used to put her up front in the aircraft and tease her in his pleasant way.

"Look, she's praying now. With all that shopping, this plane is overweight and now she's praying," he would declare theatrically. And he would laugh indulgently at this elegant woman with her many bags of designer shopping.

On her trips to London, and while in Amsterdam visiting me, my mother was in the habit of buying all manner of treasures for my brother and sister in Egypt, Nabil and Ragaa. For although she had come to visit me, my brother and sister had always been her favourites. I don't know why this was so. Was it because I was an accident? Or could it have been my mother compensating because of the additional attention my father had always given to me?

Whatever the reason, the fact had never particularly bothered me because I had always benefited from being my father's chosen child. I still adored my mother, of course, even though the love she handed out was not always equally distributed.

During the twelve years since my father's death in 1967, the anger I had felt at being excluded and misled about the sequence of events of that time had gradually faded. I had come to the understanding that my mother had genuinely believed she had my best interests at heart – that much was clear from her irritating determination to see me settled down, preferably with the intolerable Mona.

However, she was destined not to see her third child, the alleged 'black sheep' of the family, in such a happy situation.

For as long as I had known her, my mother had experienced problems with her kidneys. It had started out with the normal stones in the kidneys. When I was a boy, her doctor had suggested that she might benefit from drinking the natural spring water to be found in the foothills of Mount Lebanon. My father hoped he was right and so, every year, we would go for a month to Lebanon and stay near the village of Felougha in the foothills of the mountains, so my mother could drink the spring water there.

It was a very beautiful place, with dramatic scenery. The eastern shore of the Mediterranean is where the African tectonic plate collides with the Arabian plate. As a consequence, there are large mountains and of these mountain ranges, Mount Lebanon is the highest.

At a restaurant in a village called Zahlé, we would order water melon. The waiter would bring the fruit outside and cool it by placing it in the stream running down the mountain next to the restaurant. After ten minutes in the cold mountain stream it was as crisp and refreshing as an iced drink. It is a memory I have never forgotten and a world away from the heat and bustle of Beirut, just twenty-four miles away.

This was a time of relative calm in Lebanon following its independence from France in 1943 and I enjoyed our annual visits. The relative prosperity there didn't end until 1975 when the Lebanese Civil War broke out and the country was decimated. But when we used to visit it was still a paradise.

Sadly, despite our annual trips, my mother's kidney problems continued to worsen as the years went by. My father lived in hope that the spring water would help her.

Now we know that barley is very good for the kidneys; my mother should probably have had a few beers instead, but that was definitely not her style.

When my mother arrived to visit me in June 1974 she clearly was not well. She had been staying in London but as soon as I met her at the airport in Amsterdam I knew something was wrong. She was very short of breath and seemed confused.

I took her to see my GP, Dr Paul Sabel.

He didn't seem too concerned.

"I think she's just a bit jet-lagged," he concluded after examining her. This struck me as rather unlikely as there is only one hour's difference in time between London and Amsterdam, and she had been in London for a few weeks already.

I was still very worried, so the next day I took my mother to a private hospital, the Vrije University Medical Centre in Amsterdam. Hospitals in Holland tend to be faith based, but the university college hospitals were free from that, and this one had an excellent reputation. Things happened very fast as soon as she arrived. A shunt was put in her thigh and she was given dialysis to clear the uric acid from her blood.

My mother was sixty-five and I understand she was a borderline case for dialysis because of the strain the procedure puts on the heart.

But after treatment, and as she lay recuperating in a bed in the hospital, she seemed much more like her usual self and said she was happy I had arranged the private treatment for her.

I spent a lot of time with her in the hospital, sitting with her and talking. She was full of gratitude that I was caring for her.

"You are the one I've been neglecting these past few years, and yet you are the one who is looking after me," she said, full of wonder, as we held hands.

In the afternoon the day after she was admitted to hospital, we ended up talking – inevitably – about romance. She had met Cory M on her last visit of course, and I thought it was time to change the subject before she started talking to me about the many virtues of Mona.

"When you met my father, was he the love of your life?" I found myself asking her.

"Oh no," she told me, breezily. "There was a headmaster, Mr Chukery, who taught at the school where my brother was a teacher. I was madly in love with him. I waited for him for two years but he did not propose."

I was astonished to hear this.

"I've always thought that you loved my father," I exclaimed.

"Oh no, not exactly. I liked him, I respected him, I loved him to a certain extent, but my real love was reserved for the head teacher, Chukery," she said with a gentle smile.

She told me how he used to talk to her and say, "I wish you would be my wife" but stopped short of a formal proposal. In Egypt when my mother was growing up these things were still handled in a very formal way. You didn't just jump into bed with a girl. Instead, after talking to one another and coming to an understanding, a man would go and see the girl's father. But this headmaster had stopped short of this crucial step.

My mother looked wistful for a moment, "Your father was fine, he looked after me and was always very kind, but my real love was Mr Chukery."

It was such a personal thing to tell me. What she had said did not concern me at all. What I really loved was the fact that she had opened her heart to me. It meant she trusted me implicitly, and that meant a great deal.

Two days after this revelatory conversation, my mother passed away. I believe the dialysis was too much for her heart and it failed.

I was terribly upset and I was also very disappointed with my brother and my sister. They were living close to her and must have known how ill she was, yet still they let her travel and had not said a word to me.

After she died I phoned my sister to tell her the news and explained that I would arrange to have her body sent home to Cairo.

"Oh Nazie, just bury her anywhere," were my sister's words. I was so offended because we have a private burial ground in Old Cairo – our own place – but neither of my siblings, as it turned out, seemed to care.

I carried on regardless. It was important to me to do the right thing.

Our mother needed to be embalmed before she could be transported to Cairo and that meant buying a heavy coffin with a lead lining to preserve her body during repatriation.

I then arranged to accompany her back to Egypt. It was a big funeral. All my uncles were so grateful that I had brought her home.

"Nazie, you've done so well. We're proud of you. Thank you so much for bringing our sister back," one of them told me, and the others said similar things.

I know I did the right thing for her. And it gave me peace in some way, having been excluded from my father's death.

However, it continued to upset me for a long while that the people my mother had devoted her life to appeared not to have minded whether she came back to Cairo, or not. They had been her favourites but she died with me.

I did not talk to my brother and sister for a long time after that.

Chapter Nine

RED HAIR AND
A FIERY TEMPER

❧

*Women are like tea bags. You never know
how strong they are until they're in hot water –
Eleanor Roosevelt*

Working as British Caledonian's ticket desk
supervisor at Schiphol Airport in 1975 was a petite
Scottish girl with a shock of red hair, a scatter of
freckles and lively blue-grey eyes. Patricia also had a
Dutch boyfriend with whom she was very much in
love. They had met while he was in the Royal
Netherlands Navy, which had moored near Glasgow
for a while as part of a NATO squadron. Peter was
Patricia's first serious boyfriend and when he came
back home to Amsterdam she had followed him.

Patricia was only twenty-one and had a lovely smile and a cheeky sense of humour. We'd first met in 1973 at British Caledonian's office in town, shortly after I'd arrived in Amsterdam. I was there for a meeting and was in the lift with Robbie, a friend who would later become my best friend as well as Station Manager for the airline in Amsterdam.

On one floor the lift stopped and a girl wearing a rust-coloured two-piece suit got in. She turned around and waited for the lift to start moving. In a stage-whisper, Robbie said he would give me a six-pack of beer if I dared to pinch her bottom. That was easy. I did that.

On the way out of the lift she turned around and said in a Scottish accent, slightly pink cheeks and with her freckled nose stuck in the air, "You bad devil". Robbie and I laughed our heads off. I found out later that when she mentioned our shameless behaviour to her boss in the accounts department, he advised her to keep well away from both of us; well, he was a Jehovah's Witness. Anyway, we left her alone for a bit because we knew she was hooked up with the Dutch guy.

By 1975 Patricia was working at Schiphol Airport and was in charge of ticketing and sales.

She clearly wasn't interested in me, but I liked her. Sometimes the children came to the airport with me to watch the planes, and we always went to see

Patricia at the ticket desk. My daughter Samantha liked to sit there and scribble on the bits of paper that Patricia would give her.

Ferdy was five and she always made him laugh by pulling funny faces and saying silly things in her Scottish accent. She had a fantastic sense of humour but I was also intrigued because she seemed rather proper; it was clear she'd led a rather protected life and had had a sheltered childhood. I used to like to go in the lift with her and tease her, just to see if I could make her Scottish reserve slip a little. I'm sure she knew that recent events meant I'd earned myself something of a reputation and I could tell that she didn't really approve of me, but that made teasing her all the more satisfying – especially when I heard that things between her and Peter were not as rosy as they had been.

One night, we had a cancelled flight and I offered to give her a lift home as it was rather late.

I knew that if I just asked her outright she would probably turn me down, so I came up with a ruse. When a flight is cancelled, the food for the passengers has to be disposed of. It can't be given to an old peoples' home or an orphanage, as you might expect, because of the time limit on the freshness of the food and the accompanying risk of food poisoning, so I grabbed a bag of bread rolls and made my move.

"I want to feed the ducks in the canals. Will you come with me?"

It was midnight but Patricia's eyes sparkled. She seemed to think this was a great idea and there was something childlike about her enthusiasm.

I decided to gild the lily a little.

"Why don't you leave your car at the airport? You have to work tomorrow morning at six, and so do I. Why not leave the car here and I'll drive you home and pick you back up in the morning?"

She didn't look too happy about that, so I smiled and added, "Don't worry, we're only going to just throw this food to the ducks and then I'll drop you home."

We drove to the forest, fed the ducks and kissed. Just kissed.

At that point I did not know that she would become Mrs El Masry the second. She may have been tiny, but she was wily and she was very clever. Patricia knew how to get rid of any competition.

She did it with humour, and a furious temper. I was very fond of Cory, but she was very serious compared to Patricia, who always made me laugh.

I also liked the way that Patricia was quite reserved with me and that I knew my place here; I had been nothing more than the standby when things had gone wrong with Peter. Scottish people don't fall over themselves to be affectionate, which certainly got my attention.

But to begin with, I didn't really take the relationship seriously and continued to see other girls including Cory and, from time to time, at my mother's insistence, the insufferable Mona.

While I was friends with Patricia she'd met Mona and told me she didn't care for her. I wouldn't have expected Patricia to like her, because by this point I think she had started to like me herself, but it went deeper than that. I think she instinctively did not trust her.

And so it was that my relationship with Mona came to an end the day she turned up in Holland with her luggage and announced she was moving in. My family wanted me to marry her, however this was the straw that broke this particular camel's hump.

Soon I had found out that Mona's intention was to get rid of my maid, send the children away to boarding school and live happy-ever-after, just the two of us. She knew I was no angel and I felt she wanted to muscle into my life, remove my children and get rid of my friends.

I put Mona up in a hotel and she left Amsterdam the following day. Just a few months later she married a toy-boy and gave him a son. I was so happy for her. And happy for me that I had escaped her elegantly manicured clutches.

Patricia seemed relieved, and not only for herself.

She genuinely cared about the children. But she did have to put up with a lot.

Once, when Patricia and I were only just getting to know each other, she asked if she could visit Chart. This was a lovely little cottage on the corner of two quiet roads that I had bought in Horley, after I sold my semi-detached house in Haroldsea Drive in 1973.

A few days before Patricia arrived I'd invited Cory M to spend a few days with me there too. I generally planned these slightly duplicitous assignations carefully, but on this occasion I hadn't seen the note that Cory had left in the kitchen which read, "Thank you for a lovely few days, I enjoyed them tremendously".

When Patricia saw the note she went mad. She got hold of my electric razor and she lobbed it at me overarm. I ducked. The front door happened to be open and this high-speed missile bounced off the bonnet of Johnny Elmer's Rolls-Royce which was parked right outside.

"Bloody hell," he yelled as the razor came flying past. He was the father of one of my friends and had just arrived at the house; he jumped back into his car and quickly drove away.

Patricia hadn't finished. Screaming at me, she got hold of my trousers and ripped them up the crotch – I was lucky not to still be in them. What a performance-

and-a-half. It was like a trip to London's West End without the need to buy a ticket.

No-one in my life had ever stood up to me the way that Patricia stood up to me that day. I already knew she had the red hair and now I saw she had the fiery temper to match. Most of the girls I had known were very easy-going, polite and no bother, but Patricia was a proper challenge who told me clearly that this behaviour was no good for the children and that what I was doing was not right in her eyes.

All this was happening while she was still really not my girlfriend. I thought the eleven-year age gap meant she was too young for me, but she soon proved otherwise. She was the real strong one. Above all, my kids and maid loved her.

And once Patricia had decided I was the one for her she went flat out. I used to have a lot of parties at Gaaistraat. Patricia knew I was still going out with Cory M but she would still insist on coming over. I would always say 'okay' but after Patricia left, Cory would stay.

Patricia persisted, often quite theatrically, and her persistence meant she got gradually got rid of everybody. Soon Cory got a job with British Airways and was off the scene anyway.

I always tease Patricia that she was a one-night stand who stayed for forty years. In fact, she saw off the competition because she didn't see them as competition and most of all because she had this very, very, very nice sense of humour which I liked. But before she calmed me down she had to suffer the experience of the lovely Marian V.

One day Patricia was staying at a hotel in Copthorne, near Gatwick, on a training course. There were also some BCal crew members billeted there including Marian, a stewardess she liked, who knocked on Patricia's door and told her she'd just come back from a flight to Brazil and had lost her suitcase.

"Listen, I'm going out to dinner, do you have anything I can wear?" Marian asked her.

Immediately, Patricia offered her a velvet waistcoat, velvet trousers and a little silky blouse.

Marian was delighted. "Do you mind if I borrow these?" she asked.

"Of course not," said the very kind Patricia.

Marian came in, put the clothes on and Patricia even lent her some make-up and hairspray.

While this was going on I phoned Patricia, told her I missed her and would see her later that night. I'd also come over to Gatwick at the same time to attend to an engineering issue.

"Well don't be too late," she urged.

The lovely Patricia didn't realise she was lending Marian clothes to go out with me. She was very young and naïve. As for me it all felt like a sport. Or, as Patricia says, "It was a lot of things like that".

She was so tolerant, and she knew that eventually I had to settle down; that I couldn't go on like this. At that point I was a bit like Fred Astaire – tap, tap, tap – enjoying the dance.

Once we were back in Amsterdam I started to take Patricia more seriously. She was my friend, she was good for me and that meant gradually I got rid of the honey.

I would pick her up in my cream Mac 1 Mustang and say, "Let's go out for dinner".

I'd put Dusty Springfield's 'I Just Don't Know What to Do With Myself' on my eight-track and off we'd go to Belgium. Brussels certainly wasn't just around the corner. I went the extra mile; and an hour or two later we'd arrive there, or in Antwerp, for supper. On the way back we'd listen to Andy Williams crooning 'I Think I Love You'. It was great and the miles just flew by. That was some going on the motorways of Europe and Patricia loved it.

In 1977, when Patricia told her parents that she had "moved to Nazie's house", her father James was very grateful I had given her a room in my home. Little did he know at that point that the room was my bedroom.

When they found out we were involved, it would be fair to say that her parents were not ecstatic.

Her mother Betty did not initially like me and had stern words with Patricia when she realised that things between us were getting serious; they were aware I had a bit of a reputation, to say the least, because Patricia had told them.

"You do realise first of all, he's an Arab. Secondly, he's divorced. And, he's got two children. You're only in your early twenties," Betty cautioned her daughter, pointing out that it was a lot to take on and reminding her that she had her whole life in front of her, but Patricia wasn't daunted. She just did it and she became a wonderful stepmother to my children. She loved Ferdy and Samantha, and has always had a good relationship with them both.

Chapter Ten

FIRE AND WATER

❧

**Bravery is the capacity to perform properly
even when scared half to death – Omar Bradley**

I've always been an impulsive person. When I'm faced
with a difficult situation I am the sort of man who
generally acts without a moment's hesitation. I don't
weigh up consequences or pause to think what I should
do next. Generally, I just do it.

Such thoughts were far from my mind, however, the
day I left British Caledonian's office in the centre of
Amsterdam and walked back to my car on the other
side of the Rokin canal in the crisp spring air.

Amsterdam is an intensely pretty city with all
manner of cobbled streets, tucked away squares and
of course, its famous canals which are usually quite

busy with glass-topped barges offering scenic tours to tourists. Most people don't realise that there are more than 1200 bridges on the canals in Amsterdam.

From the water it is possible to see such attractions as the oldest surviving house in Amsterdam; a traditional merchant's house dating from 1590; and of course the seven bridges of Reguliersgracht, one of the most photographed views in Europe with its seven picturesque arched bridges receding into the distance like a set of Russian dolls and reflecting into the water below. And of course the guides always tell the tourists about the smallest house in Amsterdam which is only 6ft 8" wide.

As I left the office and walked over the small arched bridge right outside, I paused for a moment at the top to watch one of these barges gliding beneath with its commentary blaring.

A woman was standing next to me on the bridge looking at the view. Her daughter, who must have been about three or four years old, was sitting atop a stone pillar at the apex of the bridge. I was just about to continue my walk to the car when I heard a cry and turned to see the girl falling into the canal. It was at least eighteen feet to the surface of the water; a long way for a little girl to fall. She landed with a terrific splash and disappeared beneath the silty surface.

Instinctively, I threw off my linen jacket, kicked off

both leather shoes and jumped into the water after her. This is my trouble, I don't think, I act.

The water was filthy and full of mud. I'm only an average swimmer but I was able to grab her and swim with her to the edge of the canal while her hysterical mother shouted her name.

I pulled the little girl onto the cobbled pavement and her mother wrapped her up in her coat and cried tears of relief. I waited with them, dripping foul-smelling water onto the pavement, while a nearby shopkeeper called the police. Soon the police arrived on the scene and, just as I was about to continue on my way, told me I had to go with them. They took me to the police station and, in a very sweet gesture, gave me coffee and towels while I dripped on the floor. But still they would not let me go.

It turned out they were waiting for a doctor. The worst part of this entire experience was the fact that this doctor saw fit to stick an enormous needle in my bum; Tetanus. I'd never thought about the risk of that but he explained that rats swim in the canal. Well, that was the first and last time I ever went swimming in Amsterdam. Had I known that I would have to have a tetanus injection I would never have dived in!

My inner daredevil got another airing the following year when I was returning to Amsterdam from Horley following a couple of days leave. I was travelling in the jump seat of a BAC 1-11 for the forty-five-minute scheduled flight, and chatting away to Captain Eric Saunders at 21,000 feet, when the senior stewardess burst in and told us that the forward toilet on the port side was on fire.

The toilet water heaters had a bad reputation and were known to go up in flames from time to time, a fact that BCal were very keen to keep out of the newspapers. But all the engineers on the 1-11s knew it had been a problem before.

As soon as I heard the word 'fire' instinctively I started undoing my seat belt. Stepping out of the cockpit I found myself barely able to see the toilet door. Smoke was already beginning to fill the very front of the aircraft. Staying calm, so as not to worry the few passengers nearby and cause a panic, I quickly grabbed a blanket from the overhead rack – there were no overhead lockers in the late 1970s – and bending low to avoid the smoke I unlocked the toilet door to try to locate its source.

Just as I suspected, the water heater beneath the sink unit was smouldering. Quickly, I wrapped the blanket around the boiler case before returning to the cockpit.

"Pull the circuit breaker to isolate the supply to the boiler," I instructed. I knew this would solve the problem but this needed to be done immediately to prevent the blanket from catching fire.

The captain did as requested, and soon the smoke began to dissipate. Once I was certain the blanket was not going to catch fire I locked the toilet door to ensure it stayed out of use and went back to the cockpit.

Everything had happened very quickly and the passengers didn't appear to have noticed anything was amiss.

Captain Saunders was very relieved, to say the least, and so was I. When we landed, the fire truck followed us and the captain gave the thumbs-up that all was well.

Incidents such as these were always kept out of the media, for obvious reasons.

But that night, I found myself reliving the awful events of a decade earlier when I thought Aunt Salma was trapped in a burning armchair and I was too late to save her.

Aunt Salma was the wife of my Egyptian guardian, Uncle Youssef. I was in the habit of visiting my aunt and uncle at their home in Cumberland Court, near Marble Arch, for advice on paperwork or merely just to be sociable and eat and drink together. Aunt Salma was a very sweet woman who always told me stories of her romance with Uncle Youssef.

At this point, London's Covent Garden was still a fully functioning fruit and vegetable market and was to remain so until November 1974 when it was relocated to a purpose-built seventy-acre site at Nine Elms, near Waterloo Station. I was always looking for ways to save money and used to go early to buy produce at wholesale prices.

At its height the market was the destination for almost a third of all the fruit and vegetables imported into the country and it was the premier price-setting market in Britain. Products were shipped in from places like California, Marrakesh and Holland, and trucked in overnight from as far as the border with Scotland.

I was at the market early in the morning. It was an exciting and busy place where men were untying ropes from canvas sheets and unloading everything from onions to water melons onto the cobbles. The air was full of the wonderful smells of fruit and frying bacon.

Making my way past the stalls selling breakfast and cups of tea to the busy workers, I reached a wholesaler selling grapes. There were boxes and boxes of them. Grapes were still an occasional and expensive treat in the 1960s and worth getting excited about.

I picked up five or six cartons.

Uncle Youssef loved seedless grapes, so I phoned to ask if he would like some.

"Oh yes, we would love some," he responded enthusiastically.

"Great, I'll drop them in later," I said.

After I'd finished work I called my aunt.

"I'll be with you in an hour or so with the grapes," I said.

"Alright, *chérie*, come up, Youssef is out but I'll be here," she said — she was Egyptian and had been brought up the French way; French culture exists strongly in Egypt and dates back at least to Napoleon Bonaparte's arrival in the late eighteenth century.

I drove to Cumberland Court in Marble Arch, parked my car on the street in front of the smart brick and stone residential building where they lived on an upper storey, picked up a carton of the grapes, went inside and pressed the button to call the lift.

A few moments later I heard footsteps coming down the stairs around the corner, followed by a commotion as people began running into the lobby.

"Fire! Fire!" they were shouting.

I took no notice. I certainly couldn't see any flames. I continued to wait for the lift, and after its scissor doors had slowly and noisily opened, I stepped inside.

The lift creaked its way up to the fifth floor, where my uncle and aunt lived, and it was then I began to smell smoke. As the lift brought me to eye level with the floor I saw smoke pouring from under the door of Uncle Youssef's apartment.

The doors of the lift seemed to take an age to open.

I ran out of the lift and put down the grapes. I tried to open the door but it was locked.

I didn't know what else to do so I took a run up, with my shoulder to the fore, and slammed into the door like they do in old movies. It didn't budge. I tried again, my heart pounding at the thought of Aunt Salma trapped inside and unable to get out. It was a solid wooden door and I'm not a very big person, so don't ask me how I did it, but at the second attempt the door came off his hinges and slammed to the floor.

I ran down the smoke-filled corridor, pushed open the door at the far end and was confronted with the sight of a burning armchair. My eyes were full of smoke and tears.

I was certain Aunt Salma was in the chair which was now an inferno of leaping flames.

I remembered that there were fire extinguishers in little glass boxes in each of the stairwells, so I ran back down the corridor and onto the landing, smashed the glass with my elbow and pulled out the nearest one.

I dashed back into the apartment. It was still full of smoke and by this time the curtains had gone up in the inferno. The heat was intense and it was very difficult to see clearly. The chair was still burning and I went wild with the fire extinguisher, aiming it at the chair which I couldn't see clearly for smoke, and trying very hard to put the fire out.

My eyes were still pouring with tears and smoke when I heard the firefighters arrive behind me.

"All right, lad. Let's take over," the chief said as I was bundled out of the apartment, feeling appalled that I had not been able to save Aunt Salma.

In fact, she had not been sitting in the chair at all. She had a reputation for forgetfulness and had decided to walk across Hyde Park to go shopping in Harrods, overlooking entirely the fact that I was on my way.

Aunt Salma was also a smoker, and she was in the habit of leaving an ashtray on the armrest of her armchair. It turned out that a smouldering cigarette had fallen out of the ashtray and on to the seat cushion. Her absentmindedness again; she thought she'd put it out. Unfortunately, the chair was upholstered in hessian which was like a giant wick and the whole thing had caught alight.

My uncle was grateful for my help in putting out the fire, as were the fire department who pointed out that the entire building might have burned down if I hadn't arrived at that moment with a carton of grapes. Thankfully, I had thought Aunt Salma would be home or I would have left the grapes with the concierge.

In fact, the chief was so happy with me that he invited me to spend a day undertaking basic fire training.

It was on this course that he told me a simple rule,

which is now widely known but was less well known then.

"If you are confronted by fire always crawl on your belly. Smoke rises. If you crawl you will be able to see a lot better than you can when standing up and you'll still be able to breathe," he explained.

It is a rule I have never forgotten and which I remembered during the toilet fire on the BAC 1-11.

And as for Aunt Salma, when she arrived back from shopping to find her apartment had been incinerated, the firefighter gave her merry hell. "You should stop smoking," he boomed. "You nearly burned the block down."

My other memorable experience of setting off a fire extinguisher was on a Vickers Viscount. It was the first mistake I made as a fledgling aircraft engineer working for BUA in my coat with a red collar, signifying my subordinate status as a junior licensed technician.

Hugh Morgan was Senior Engineer and shift leader that day.

My job was simple enough. I had to sit in the cockpit and keep my finger on the low pressure valve while they bled the plane's engine. I was looking out of the window on to the tarmac and awaiting the thumbs-up from Hugh to tell me that the system had been bled –

my cue to check whether the figure on the read-out was correct.

Unfortunately, my attention wandered and when it was time to press the low pressure valve a second time to recalibrate the reading I accidentally pressed the fire extinguisher button that is located next to it.

The fire extinguisher made a terrific whooshing sound that I could hear even from the calm of the cockpit. It was followed very rapidly by a second sound; that of the electricians and engineers who had just been doused in foam. I wasn't popular at all on that occasion.

When it comes to flying, it is true that today it is one of the safest forms of travel. It is said to be safer than going by car to the airport. It wasn't always so in the past. The problem is that when something goes wrong it is so dramatic.

When you handle a plane you treat it like eggs. And what is so sad is when occasionally you have a pilot with depression who drives it deliberately into a mountain. In one such case, in March 2015, Andreas Lubitz, the co-pilot of Germanwings Flight 9525 – a low-cost carrier owned by Lufthansa – locked the captain out of the cockpit and flew into the French Alps, sixty miles from Nice.

Lubitz had previously been treated for suicidal

tendencies and declared "unfit to work" by a doctor but he kept this information from ops (Flight Operations). It was only after he had killed himself and 149 other people by initiating a controlled descent that continued until the aircraft impacted in the mountains, that the medical certificate was found in a bin.

I have never forgotten the aftermath of what I saw following the fatal air accident at Gatwick on 5th January 1969 when a Boeing 727 with sixty-two people on board crashed into a house on its approach to Gatwick in heavy fog. Due to pilot error, the flaps were not extended to maintain flight at final approach speed.

It was a foggy night and I woke up, on a day off, to a dreadful booming sound.

"Hi, this is Nazie. What the hell was that?" I said after I'd grabbed the phone and called ops.

"We're not sure Nazie, but we think it was an Ariana Afghan Airline flight that was trying to come in, though we didn't hear anything from the pilot."

I dressed quickly and drove to the Balcombe road. I should never have gone. What I saw is still in my mind. Bodies everywhere and people dying.

There was no auto-land at that time and the plane had come in low, hitting trees and chimneys on several houses before colliding with a large detached house which it demolished, before catching fire. Forty-eight passengers and crew died, and two adult occupants of the house were killed when it was destroyed by the impact. A baby in the house survived with minor injuries.

Although big commercial jets are a lot easier to fly now than in the past – automation and GPS technology have made the process akin to flying a giant computer – when something does go wrong it is generally a result of the autopilot being disengaged.

When you have an emergency, such as an engine failure or hydraulic issue, rule number one is to keep the plane in autopilot so you can deal with the problem. However, the temptation is to disconnect the autopilot and fly manually. And that's why, when something goes wrong, it is generally pilot error.

There are red books in the cockpit of commercial jets that have been written by senior, more experienced pilots who know what to do in every eventuality. In nine out of ten incidents when something goes wrong, the pilots have not been following correct procedure.

Chapter Eleven

SHALL WE GET MARRIED?

❧

Don't ask anyone to do a job that you have not already tackled yourself – Anon

Soon after we started living together in 1977, Patricia and I decided to go on a world trip. We flew to New York a few months after Jimmy Carter, a peanut farmer from Georgia, became the thirty-ninth President of the United States on 20th January 1977.

The night we arrived we heard fireworks from our hotel room at the Sheraton and thought it was a celebration. The following morning at breakfast we asked a diner on the next table whether he'd heard the display too?

"No," he said, "That wasn't fireworks, that was shooting".

New York was lawless at that time and had a reputation as 'Fear City', a name its own police force had given it. Later we found out that people were killed in the streets that night.

While we were away Patricia cut her hair *à la garçon*. The very short fringe really suited her and my little Scottish pixie looked very *à la mode*.

The children stayed with their mother and grandmother in the UK while we visited the best hotels in San Francisco, Hawaii, Manila, Tokyo, Malaysia and Singapore.

I had a little treat in store for Patricia during the three weeks we were away – in each of these destinations I would arrive at reception and ask to talk to the front office manager.

He would come bustling out and I would say, discreetly, "May I have a word?"

"Of course, Sir," he would answer.

"I don't want to make a scene but we're honeymooners. Is there any chance of an upgrade?"

"Of course," he would declare. "And may I offer my congratulations to you and your lovely wife?"

And we got the honeymoon suite, on the house, at

every hotel we stayed at, all around the world. Patricia loved that too.

The following year we took the children to Florida, where we met up with my cousin Ezzat and his wife Nadia who lived in Baltimore, Maryland. We were staying at the Hilton St Petersburg Bayfront and the children were playing on the beach. It was a beautiful day; not for nothing is St. Petersburg nicknamed the 'Sunshine City'. Ferdy was going to be eleven in a couple of weeks and Samantha was seven-and-a-half. Everyone was happy.

It was also the eleventh anniversary of my father's death. I always remember him especially keenly on the 11th July every year. Generally, my father is always in the forefront of my mind for his advice and his suggestions; everything I do, he's there. But on this particular day I believed I knew what he would want. As to my mother, I was quite certain she would have approved of the next big step I was about to take.

Patricia was perched on her sun lounger reading a novel under the shade of a sun umbrella to protect her very fair skin.

I turned to her. "Shall we get married?"

The look on her freckled face was a picture to behold.

"Yes, Nazie," she said calmly. "I'd like that."

She'd been on at me for months, of course. I'd made it quite clear that there would be a condition; no more kids. I was quite happy with the two we had.

But being me, and impulsive to the core, I added that I wanted to get married right there and then; on the 11th July; the eleventh anniversary of my father's death.

"I do want to get married, Nazie, but only if we can get married by a priest," she insisted. Being a Catholic, a registry office was out. Soon Nadia, my cousin's wife, had at my urging got a copy of the St. Petersburg Yellow Pages and looked up 'wedding officiants'. Life is quite easy if you approach things in this way, always believing that things will work out. And it turned out to be even better than that.

"Here's one who's quite nearby," said Nadia as she ran her finger down the page back in our hotel room. "His name is Lucien Behar".

I nearly fell off my chair. "Lucien Behar! I was at school with him in Cairo."

I phoned him up and he couldn't believe it either. We made an appointment to meet at his parish.

It turned out that we had to wait three days to get married because at that time in America you had to have a blood test.

Patricia is a bit squeamish. She held out her thumb so the doctor at a clinic near the hotel could take blood.

"No madam, roll your sleeve up."

Her freckled face was a picture.

"No way," she said, looking at me with that steely glint that she gets in her flint-blue eyes when she isn't happy.

"You want to get married or not?" I replied. "If you want to get married, roll your sleeve up. If you don't want to get married, we'll go away."

From the expression on her face you would have thought she was having her left arm amputated.

Lucien Behar married us three days after the anniversary of my father's death, on 14th July 1978. Patricia was twenty-four. I was thirty-five. Lucien's wife Molly was delighted to be a witness, together with my cousin Ezzat. That evening we invited them over and had a nice party with the children, who were very happy that Daddy and Patricia were now a married couple. And Lucien had a wedding present for us; the omission of the marriage fees.

When we returned from the United States, Patricia broke the news to her parents that we had got married and, with the help of her elder sister, we were able to convince them that this was the best thing for their daughter.

Once they had accepted the marriage they travelled to Holland with various gifts from the whole family. I ended getting on very well with her parents; her father in particular had a very good sense of humour and that, of course, was what had first attracted me to his daughter.

Our wedding certificate still makes Patricia and me laugh now. The clerk was an African American and very, very dark skinned. On the line on the wedding certificate where she was required to describe the racial heritage of the two individuals getting married, she filled it in as follows; Colour – White.

This was the first and perhaps the last time my Arabian skin tones have been described in such a way.

Chapter Twelve

GEORGE THE GHOST

❧

***Do not take life too seriously. You will never
get out of it alive – Elbert Hubbard.***

There they were again. Footsteps.

It sounded like someone was walking very slowly
down the corridor towards our bedroom. This was the
third night that the muffled thump of footsteps had
woken me up.

Patricia was asleep, so I knew it couldn't be her.

I switched on the bedside light, as I had on the
previous two occasions, but of course there was no-one
there.

I waited. Then they started up again. Thump,
thump, thump.

Later that morning I phoned my estate agent, Chris

O'Malley, the Irishman who'd sold me the house a few weeks earlier and who I used to see sometimes in the Half Moon in Charlwood for a drink after work.

"Chris, what the hell is that noise?" I asked.

"Oh, that's George. You don't have to worry about him, he's harmless," he replied in his breezy Irish way.

I thought he was talking nonsense; ghosts, there is no such thing. Yet strange things had been happening since we'd moved to Valetta.

The house was a rambling four-bedroom Tudor place right next door to Chart, the pretty cottage we'd just sold to a retired couple who wanted it so much they had asked us to name our price.

Together with my generous salary, this had enabled us to buy Valetta, which was to be our English home for the next eight years or so.

After we'd exchanged contracts on Valetta, Chris had given me a set of keys in case we needed to measure up for carpets or curtains.

It turned out that the date of completion of the sale did not suit my roster in Amsterdam. When I realised I wasn't going to be in the UK the day the house became ours I hatched a plan.

A few weeks before completion, Patricia and I, together with our Dutch friend Louis Goessen, flew to the UK to carry out an important and covert task under cover of darkness. After what would be our last dinner at Chart, and when it was dark, we turned out the lights and crept into the garden. Keeping as quiet as possible, we carefully unscrewed a section of the wooden fence that separated it from Valetta. In the dead of night, we then moved all our furniture and possessions through the garden and in through the back door of our soon-to-be-new-home, assuming no-one would be any the wiser.

This plan backfired when a few days later Chris left a message to say the owner had asked for a final inspection of her property before the completion date.

I called Chris back and told him what we had done. I'm sure he almost fell off his chair.

"I've been an estate agent for thirty-three years and this has never, ever happened before, Naz," he exclaimed. "What the hell am I going to tell her?"

"Just tell her the truth," I said.

He did and a couple of weeks later we completed and all was well, but for a while we were the talk of Horley.

Valetta was a huge place. The four bedrooms were each decorated in a different colour; so we had the red room, the pink room, the green room and so on. There were also five bathrooms, a dining room, a drawing room, and two garages.

It was clear that George the ghost favoured the

green bedroom, which was positioned over the integral garage.

One night as I was walking up the stairs I felt certain there was someone watching me. Things got more peculiar when I reached the top of the stairs, walked along the corridor and turned into our bedroom. It was then that I felt a breath on the back of my neck. I nearly jumped out of my skin.

"Fucking hell," I cried out. "What the hell is that?"

I went to find Patricia. "It's happened again, and this time he was breathing down my neck". She laughed and so did I, but the question remained; was the house really haunted?

That night I went down to the pub to have another drink with Chris.

"Okay, not only does the guy knock, I feel he's breathing down my neck – literally," I explained. "What the hell is going on?"

Chris laughed. "Honestly he's harmless. Don't worry about George." We drank up and had a good evening.

I'd always had an understanding with Patricia that if I drank too much at the pub I would call a taxi and stay in a hotel near the airport. However, I would also do this if I had flown into the UK for one night only and didn't want to open the house up for such a short stay while Patricia was at our home in Amsterdam.

But I always made a point of teasing Patricia that I was staying in the hotel because of the haunting presence of George – and she believed me. Of course, I wasn't really going to let a ghost, real or imagined, get the better of me.

Next time we were in England we set about sorting out the house to our requirements and arranged to have new carpets laid throughout. I nearly bled to death when I took matters into my own hands after the carpet fitter had finished the job and I noticed that he had missed a bit under the step outside Samantha's bedroom. Being a 'macho man' I insisted on finishing the job. How hard could it be to use one of those curved knives – he'd used it, why not me?

I got hold of one and I severed my artery. As I said, I never was any good with tools, it's why I was made a supervisor rather than a mechanic when I started with BUA.

Blood was pouring out of me. Patricia bundled me in to the car with the children and drove us all to A&E where I was stitched up.

Ferdy and Samantha were in the waiting room and I waved to them through an internal window to reassure them that Daddy was alright. And all of a sudden a great gush of blood poured out while I was waving.

The doctor was very embarrassed.

"Get out, get out," he said to the nurses. And then he did it properly.

I still have the scar to this day.

Meanwhile, the situation with George was still going on. The 'footsteps' continued for the best part of a year until finally I thought I had better sort this 'ghost' out.

Before going to bed, I would put the heating on and I discovered that because it was a long way from the boiler to the green room, air pockets in the pipes were creating a sound reminiscent of someone walking in the corridor.

But what about the slight draught I had felt?

In the green bedroom I discovered an old air vent that had been sealed with paper, and which had a slight tear.

When the heating system was on, the paper was gently sucking in and out. The movement of the paper created a gentle draught similar to someone breathing on one's neck.

George's existence was very much an engineering issue, not a paranormal one, but I didn't tell Patricia that.

Next time I saw Chris at the pub I told him that George wasn't real, after all. He was a bit disappointed.

"Do you know these houses sell for a fortune when they have a ghost in residence?" he said.

"Well, if you can keep a secret, I will," I laughed. And together we did.

Eventually we sold the house to a lady who turned it into a bed-and-breakfast, and I wouldn't be surprised if the legend of the ghost persists to this day.

When I finally told Patricia the truth she laughed her head off, but we still remain very fond of old George.

Chapter Thirteen

LEATHER JACKETS AND FRENCH BEANS

❧

Be honest with yourself. Be punctual, never give up, achieve your goals, even when everything goes bad – Steve Jobs

Who says engineers generally do not make good businessmen? Probably the same people who claim they do not make good salesmen either. And, generally speaking, they are probably right.

Among my aeronautical colleagues were commodity dealers, car dealers, people dealing in aircraft parts – everything from landing gear to toilet roll dispensers and drinks trolleys – and others with a finger in every type of money-making scheme imaginable, but not many of those who successfully diversified by starting a business were engineers.

In those days at least, engineers tended to have less imaginative capacity than pilots, perhaps because they tended to be older, RAF-trained, and not prepared to think too far beyond the enormous responsibility of keeping these man-made birds flying.

Most pilots, however, had sidelines because they were permitted only about a 110 flying hours per month, giving them more free time. If they were flying long-haul, this meant they often did a lot of those hours at the start of the month leaving them with two or even three weeks off every four weeks or so.

This was fertile ground for all manner of extra-curricular employment.

Take Captain Robin Brodie James, for example, with his hill of Christmas trees near Christchurch, Dorset. Every year, at the end of November, he would take three weeks off and go with his brother to cut his crop, ready for seasonal sale, before putting his BCal pilot's stripes back on again before Christmas.

As for Captain Robbie Robinson, whom Patricia rather fancied, he had a spring at the bottom of his garden. Long before the era of mass-produced bottled water, Robinson was bottling his spring water and selling it to local supermarkets.

Every time I got talking to the pilots they seemed to have something on the go.

Having said that, there were also a lot of them who

would spend most of their free time in the pub. They would be there every morning, drinking until lunch time and back again in the evening to conclude the day with another couple of rounds.

I was younger than my RAF-trained engineering colleagues, I was hungry, and I learned to diversify from the pilots, but although I wanted to do something away from aviation I always fell on my face when I did. Despite my early success with Auto Line, I hadn't yet learned an important lesson; true success comes from dealing in what you know, not merely what's on offer.

However, every self-made businessman has to start somewhere.

For Sir Richard Branson it was selling records from a church, having had his own failed Christmas tree experiment at the age of thirteen when rabbits ate the 400 saplings he had planted from seed in a Sussex field.

For consumer electronics wizard Lord Alan Sugar, it was selling electrical knick-knacks, including car aerials, out of a van that he had bought for £50.

For diamond magnate Laurence Graff, it was working as a fifteen-year-old apprentice at a Hatton Garden jewellery shop, before selling his own designs when the shop went bust.

As for me, I started my international aviation

spares business by dealing in nothing less than a load of leather jackets and crate of canned French beans.

It was David Bryantson, my friend from Horley and former business partner who had shared the Auto Line office, who offered me the jackets. Made of top quality hide, the price was very attractive and the two samples he showed me looked perfect. I made some enquiries and there seemed to be a lot of potential.

I thought I could sell quite a few of these to my many contacts. I hired a van and purchased all 250 pieces on offer from a warehouse near Gatwick airport. It was always money up front with these lads so I paid them in cash.

As soon as I got home I picked up the phone and by lunchtime had sold ten of them to friends who promised to buy more soon. I was busy selling jackets by word of mouth for the next few days – hearsay is the most powerful way to sell anything and it was not very difficult.

That was until my customers started calling me back. Apparently there was a serious problem with the jackets. I took one out of its plastic wrapping and tried it on. It was cut upside down, with the waist larger than the shoulders. I grabbed another one and held it up to the first; the same problem. And again with the third and the fourth. Bloody hell. They were all cut upside down.

When you put them on there was a swathe of extra leather at the back – perfect for a body like the Hunchback of Notre Dame, but no good at all for my clients.

I started giving refunds and agonised about how I was going to get my money back. It was a very stressful time, money was tight and I had to find a way to get rid of the damn jackets.

Fortunately, Wim Van Rai, a friend of Patricia's, had an unconventional solution in the form of a twenty-foot container of canned French beans at his place near Utrecht. He was prepared to exchange all the beans for all the jackets.

All it took was for Pete Damen, a Dutch friend of mine who worked at Schiphol Airport, to drive the jackets from Horley to Holland in my Volkswagen van once Wim had a client lined up.

A trader to his core, Wim was involved in numerous money-making deals. The problem with the jackets didn't put him off, he was still able to flip them – sell them on – and turn a profit. Naturally, he got a cut from both ends of the deal. When he flipped the jackets he made money. When he flipped the beans he made money. He had his finger in every pie. He wouldn't tell me his plans for the jackets, but I reckon he sold them on to someone who was planning to cut the sleeves off and turn them into waistcoats.

Beans for coats; you have to find a way to fill the gaps to come out of a bad transaction clean.

When things go wrong, don't despair, move on. It's always been my mantra. But I had never seen so many French beans under one roof – there were crates of the things.

I sold them cheap, again using the most effective sales technique known to man – word of mouth – and I kept on selling until there wasn't a single can of the beans left. Pilots, cabin staff, neighbours and friends; everyone I knew bought a few cans. They loved the product and I made sure they loved the price.

In the end, Patricia and I came out of the debacle of the jackets and the beans having made a very small profit, but we had learned a great deal more.

The secret is never to give up when it all goes wrong. If I hadn't followed that advice I wouldn't be where I am today.

Chapter Fourteen

A BRAND NEW BABY

❧

*It takes twenty years to build a reputation and
five minutes to ruin it. If you think about that,
you'll do things differently – Warren Buffett*

When Patricia and I married it had been on the clear
understanding that there were to be no more children.
But when Julian Marcus El Masry, my third child and
second son, was born on 29th March 1982, everything
changed.

I could have had a thousand more Julians and I was
so glad I had allowed myself to be persuaded into
fatherhood for a third time at the age of thirty-nine.

Conceived in Dallas, Texas, and born in
Amsterdam, his was the first natural birth I had seen
and even after sixteen hours of fighting, screaming
and yelling, Patricia felt the same way.

"Nazie, I wouldn't mind having another," she said, to my astonishment, as she cradled her newborn son in her arms.

From that point on, Patricia and Julian were joined at the hip, and remain so conjoined to this day. Their bond became especially intense because when he was eight months old Julian was diagnosed with asthma.

In the early months we were back and forth to the hospital in the middle of the night for him to receive oxygen. These were anxious days when we barely slept, taking turns to pace around the house with him in an attempt to soothe him as he leaned into our shoulders for comfort.

I used to do an hour-and-a-half and then I would hand him over to Patricia and she would do an hour-and-a-half. Sometimes I would drive him around in the early hours in an attempt to try to help him sleep.

In the early eighties, the treatment for asthma was more primitive than it is now. Ventolin, the modern rescue medicine of choice, was approved the year Julian was born but it wasn't available as an inhaler until later in the 1980s. And it wasn't to be until 1989 that the focus changed from treating the symptoms to controlling asthma with preventative medicine.

Thankfully pharmacology has moved on. But at the time we were so busy with the task of trying to keep Julian healthy that there was no time to have other children.

There was also the question of our fledgling business which we had set up a few months before Julian's birth.

Over the years, I had continued to use my time at work very efficiently. Being a defects engineer enabled me to ensure I had a lot of spare time by closely following the planes and anticipating when I would be required. If I knew a plane had been delayed in Milan, for example, I would look up its history and be waiting at the airport to sort it out.

The spare time this diligence created was coupled with an idea I'd had for a business. The world of aircraft components was a world I knew inside out; I had spent my working life immersed in it.

My idea was to become an independent aviation broker. If an airline needed a component I would sell it to them and only then go out and buy it. The fact that I didn't need to hold any stock meant I wouldn't need capital. In short, I was going to sell a part before I bought it.

I was convinced that 'forwarding', as this is called, was a low-risk business model which could offer great rewards. I didn't have the cash to keep spares and neither did I want any – a slightly ironic fact given that I've now got four warehouses, on three continents, covering around 400,000 square feet and inundated with components.

I was lucky because Patricia had total faith in the idea and in me. She never cautioned me or attempted to dissuade me in any way, and in time my most important cheerleader was destined to become my partner in business as well as in life.

She says she could see I was a lot happier being my own boss and she liked the fact that aviation parts was a business I could run from home. I would be able to take time off whenever I felt like it and by so doing be on hand to spend a lot of time with the family when I wasn't at the airport.

I was also aware that BCal was struggling financially and I wanted a second string to my bow. Because I was a senior engineer, and as such part of junior management, my boss Arnold – the airline's chief engineer at this point – would always talk to me about finances. Cash flow was always a problem for BCal, and it was about to get much worse. The deep instinct and urge I felt to set up my own business was not a sensation I could ignore.

When I went to see my lawyers in Horley to form my forwarding company, they had an important question to ask before we could get down to the intricacies of the paperwork.

"So, what is the name of the company," they asked as we sat around a boardroom table at their offices.

I'd been so busy focusing on the business concept that I hadn't had a moment to think about what it would be called.

Inspiration struck. I visualised the first three letters of Ferdinand and the first three letters of Samantha...

"Fersam," I said proudly. In less than two minutes our new business had a name, and a meaningful one at that.

Fersam started out as a single desk in the cellar of Gaaistraat 14, our Dutch home near Amsterdam, and we grew from there.

While Patricia looked after the books and the paperwork, I concentrated on doing the deals and sourcing the market for the spares.

The kids would go to school and we'd work on the forwarding business. I'd do a shift for BCal at Schiphol and then Patricia would do a shift in the ticketing office there. She was also in charge of BCal's rosters which helped as she could make them advantageous to our business dealings and domestic life. Frequently, we could both get ten days off at a time.

Working for BCal in Amsterdam was very easy, but with Fersam International, as we were soon calling it, we were tireless.

Patricia and I were a good team and for the next few years we worked hard to establish ourselves.

One of my earliest business mentors was a Dutch aircraft parts dealer named Guus Faber, some years older than me. We met just as I was discovering there could be a commercial value to my aeronautical engineering knowledge. But while I was focused on buying spares for aircraft, he was buying junk. Things like aircraft steps and tow bars, even the metal trolleys from which the in-flight meals are served.

"Guus, what are you buying this junk for?" I asked one day, surprised he was bothering with this stuff, mixed in with which were some valuable parts – although he didn't seem to know what they were for or how much they were worth.

He smiled. "Mr Nazie, never forget, there is somebody, somewhere in the world looking for these items, you just have to find them." I never forgot that. It was a real lesson in the art of selling.

And he had done well. One day he invited us to spend the day on his boat.

"Let's meet at the apartment first," he said. When we arrived at his home it was a poxy little place, and I thought it was very nice that he had invited us.

After a few drinks he suggested we go down to the marina and go by boat to get something to eat. And honestly, when we got there it was an incredible forty-metre long antique Dutch sailing boat; an unbelievable thing. It turned out that for nine months of the year he lived on it.

"What do I need a big apartment for?" he said. "I'm only there a couple of months a year and the rest of the time we're either on the boat or in Australia."

This was definitely a business that could fund a relaxed lifestyle. But for all the theory and aspirational dreams, we had a lot to learn.

One of Fersam's first big deals, in 1984, proved to be a white-knuckle ride; the most stressful three weeks of my life in fact. I had purchased some engine power testing equipment from the Dutch national carrier, KLM, and was feeling confident. I knew the system inside out as I had been using this large piece of machinery for years.

An engine test bed is an enclosed cabin where an aircraft engine can be tested at full power to check it is functioning correctly. This might be necessary after an engine part has been changed, to check it is operating properly, or to diagnose engine problems following a pilot report.

It is an enormous piece of kit, but when KLM contacted me to say they no longer needed the engine test equipment for their redundant fleet of DC8 aircraft and would I like to buy it, I found myself saying yes.

My industry contacts were bemused. "How on earth are you going to transport it?" one of them wanted to know.

They were right to wonder. The equipment, used for testing Pratt & Whitney JT3D engines, stood three storeys high, five-hundred-feet square and weighed thirty-five to forty tonnes.

I didn't think selling one could be all that hard but transporting it was certainly going to be a challenge, even after it was dismantled.

Things started out well after I found a customer who flew in from Miami to examine it. Bud Halwany, the owner of JetPower Services, an aerospace company that specialises in the supply of commercial aircraft engines and parts, was satisfied that the equipment was just as I had described.

Furthermore, he was willing to pay for the shipping of the machinery from Holland to Florida. There was only one problem; I had to find a way to get it to the port of Rotterdam, the largest port in Europe and at that time the world's busiest (it has now been overtaken by Singapore and Shanghai). The equipment was too large and heavy to travel the twenty-five miles from Schiphol to Rotterdam by road.

But that was my problem; Bud Halwany just wanted to seal the deal. I was delighted to receive a cheque for £33,000; a lot of money in those days. It had the company logo printed on it and all seemed correct, so I did not give it another thought.

The following day, while we started dismantling the

equipment, Patricia FedExed the cheque to Barclays Bank in West Sussex, UK.

My plan was simple. I had decided to float the engine test machinery on barges from Schiphol to Rotterdam.

Nobody could believe it I was going to send the equipment by boat, but I was insistent. "We're gonna do this."

I started looking into sending shipments by canal and finding out about how to get the bridges raised for such a tall load. I do love a challenge.

Within a few days, everything was ready to go in three large containers which were lifted onto the barges.

The state police accompanied the load as it made its way along the canal system that leads out of Amsterdam to open water. Once in the sea, they were delivered safely to Rotterdam.

Then the phone rang.

It was Barclays Bank in Crawley. Slow as they are, the clerk at the bank was phoning to say that the cheque would take at least three weeks to clear. It turned out that rather than a cashier's cheque, which is signed and guaranteed by the bank, our client had given us a personal cheque which offers no such assurances. It had to be cleared by the bank before it could credit our account.

The shipment was on its way but we wouldn't know for three weeks whether it would bounce or not. If it had, we would have been in a serious financial situation.

We were due to go on holiday the following week. The vacation was ruined. I was unfamiliar with these financial complications and I couldn't sleep a wink the whole time we were away.

One of the happiest moments in my life was when the bank called a few weeks later to let me know that, finally, the cheque had cleared.

After that we opened a bank account for Fersam in the Netherlands and we soon got a lot smarter. As time went by people owed us a lot more than £33,000, but now we sleep like babies.

I may have had a deep knowledge of aviation engineering, but like many young companies we made a lot of mistakes like that in the early days.

However, things always seemed to go spectacularly wrong when I stopped focusing on what I knew, which was airline parts, and got distracted by the other deals I took on in an attempt to generate funds for the aircraft parts side of the business. And of course, we were still very green. Although I had been blooded by the experience of the 'three-legged lamb' debacle two decades earlier in London, I hadn't yet learned that such brazen scams operate all the way up the business chain.

We were about to find out the hard way.

On this particular occasion we had a contact in Saudi Arabia who was seeking a contract to buy a regular container of beef luncheon meat from Europe. I approached a manufacturer near Rotterdam called Van Der Laan, which produced the stuff.

We packaged up samples and sent them to Jeddah. Word came back that the Saudis wanted to place an order for a twenty-foot container of the product on a regular basis. We were delighted. As soon as they opened a letter of credit in our name we opened a reciprocal letter of credit with our supplier – a standard technique used by intermediaries such as Fersam International to hide the identity of the actual supplier or manufacturer.

With all the paperwork in place, the first container was duly shipped to Jeddah. Upon receipt, and following standard protocol, the Saudi Ministry of Health took some samples from the tins in the container and to our dismay the meat was rejected.

The report showed that the so-called beef luncheon meat contained a high level of iodine, a clear indicator that the luncheon meat also contained pork. Worse news followed. On investigation it emerged that the Rotterdam manufacturer was also adding chicken meat and chicken skin into the mix. Our 100 per cent pure beef luncheon meat was anything but.

I contacted our lawyers and the container was destroyed in Saudi. It was a great pity because a regular twenty-foot container would have been a good little earner for us, but it served to remind us how dishonest people can be.

When it comes to probity in business, Patricia and I have always followed a very personal credo inspired in part by my father, who was a straight-shooter, and by Patricia herself who – in her typical Scottish Catholic way – cannot tell a lie.

It all started when Julian was an asthmatic baby. One day, we went to a wholesaler to buy a whipped cream dispenser for our kitchen. It was a bit of a joke we had; we used to buy delicious apple pies and always said it would be fun to be able to dispense cream like they did in restaurants. One day, instead of merely talking about it, we decided to buy one.

We stood in the wholesaler looking at two differently-sized dispensers. Big seemed better but although the smaller one had a price tag, the larger one didn't.

"There's no price on this thing," I said to Patricia. We looked around but the shop was empty and there was no-one to ask. "Oh let's just take the price off the little one and use that," I said. So we did and the very next day Julian had a severe asthma attack.

I come from a very religious family. I fear God, but I'm not as holy as my relatives are. However, I have always had a strong conscience and an inner voice telling me right from wrong. You could call it an 'elaborated conscience', away from religion of any kind. In this case I found I was not able to rest until the following visit when I spoke to the manager and admitted what I had done. I felt so relieved once I had paid the balance. A load had been lifted from my mind and I was able to feel at peace again.

This inner alarm bell is active in all areas of my life. While bringing up the children if I was ever tempted to favour one over the other – as my parents had both done – I would hear my alarm bell ringing loudly in my head, insisting on equality and fair play. And if I ever have an argument with Patricia or with one of my children I will not rest until it stops.

From then on, if ever I was tempted to fiddle a short cut to a profit, Patricia would say to me; "If you do this, Julian is going to be sick." She went one step further and believed we would actually be punished by the Almighty if we ever did anything dishonest. Although I'm not a very religious man, it is a business formula we have followed faithfully ever since.

It might sound idealistic, but with Patricia being a

Catholic and with me having grown up in such a religious household it just made sense to us.

We could have ended up dealing with military aircraft, we could have been dealing with all sorts of things – the opportunity was inevitably there as time went on and we grew our contacts – but we had a conscience and never got involved in below-board propositions. We were absolutely straight and have always been honest with everybody, and for that reason our company has a very good reputation. When dealing with something as critical as the safety of airline components, reputation is everything.

However, the canned beef folly was as nothing compared to the much more serious mistake we were about to make; doing business with a relative.

Chapter Fifteen

THE VENTURE OF THE TRUCKS

❧

***A good deal is when the vendor and the buyer
are both satisfied with it – Dougie Goldstein***

I sank gratefully into the bath. That first moment of
weightlessness briefly counteracted the stress I'd been
feeling since I had discovered, to my horror, that my
distant, so-called cousin had pushed us to the point of
bankruptcy.

I woke up to the sound of Patricia's voice.

"Nazie," she said in a whisper. "It's 6am, you've
fallen asleep in the bath again."

I'd never known tiredness like this. After my
twelve-hour shift at the airport, I'd just spent the past
eight hours on the road driving through three

countries and back again to our home in Amsterdam, where I'd arrived just after 4am. This was the third time in a week that I'd done this and I needed to be at the airport in an hour for the start of another twelve-hour shift at 7am.

My route had taken me from Amsterdam to Luxembourg, via Belgium. It was a tedious journey of just under two-hundred-and-fifty miles each way, which involved crossing the Ardennes Mountains, with the entire journey driven against the clock. For in the back of my Hertz hire truck were forty boxes of live lobsters from Sunderland. Pulled from the North Sea that morning, they would be eaten in the restaurants of landlocked Luxembourg that night.

This had been going on two or three times a week for more than a year. Normally I tried to make the trip on my days off, but sometimes it was essential to go after my shifts at the airport had finished. It was not easy. I had never been this tired before, but I was determined to pull us out of the hole in which we had found ourselves.

The trouble had started when I had agreed to go into partnership with my cousin, Kamel Wassef, the son of my London guardian Youssef.

Kamel and I had always had a close if rather strange relationship. We both enjoyed cars and used to relate at that level. He was also very generous, but in time he became rather possessive and difficult to read. He also did not like a lot of my friends. All these should have been pointers – they are certainly evidence as to why you should never go into business with family.

Kamel owned his own forwarding company at Heathrow and his business benefited from to his father's position with the newly named EgyptAir (formerly United Arab Airlines). The airline always needed forwarding agents and the deal was that Kamel would pass on some of the business to us. And what he needed were trucks to supply the cargo he was forwarding to various destinations in the UK.

His proposition, which certainly looked good on paper, was for me to supply three five-ton trucks which I would then lease to him. His company, Wetco Ltd, would make monthly payments to Fersam, and within thirty months the trucks would pay for themselves.

He was family and I trusted him, so I borrowed the money from the bank.

Kamel's company made the first few lease payments and all seemed well until Patricia was going through the bank statements for Fersam and noticed that Wetco Ltd had missed a payment.

I called Kamel up and asked what was going on. Apparently he was waiting for the airlines to pay him. It was a plausible explanation and the money duly arrived a few days later.

Then he missed another payment.

This carried on for a few more months until the day the payments stopped completely. We happened to be in London at that time and went to visit my cousin face to face. To our dismay, Kamel told us that his forwarding company had gone into receivership and our trucks had been subcontracted to Avis.

When I contacted Avis they didn't want to know; the trucks were registered with Wetco Ltd. This was a disaster. I owed the bank £23,000, a lot of money in those days. It was imperative I kept up the monthly payments to the bank to stay afloat ourselves, but how?

Our salaries with British Caledonian were enough to keep family life going, but on top of all the normal day-to-day costs we now owed a huge amount every month to Barclays in the UK. My multi-millionaire cousin had left the burden entirely on our shoulders and didn't seem prepared to help. He was clearly backed into a corner, and so were we.

As for my father, he had not of course been a businessman, but his advice was always sound and as I grew older I continued to draw upon it for guidance.

As I lay in the bath contemplating making yet another drive to Luxembourg the following night his words rang once more in my ears.

"Always make sure you pay your taxes and always

ensure you pay any money you owe to your bank, your bank will give assistance all your life if you do," he would write in his letters to me. "Your mortgage, your bank, your taxes; always have respect for those."

So that was the approach Patricia and I took when confronted by the worst financial predicament we had ever faced.

No-one, and especially not my father, would ever have guessed that the solution lay in lobsters.

While the truck situation was going on, we had been approached by a company who wanted to export live lobsters from Sunderland in the north of England to Luxembourg. We had been about to pass over the contract, but had suddenly realised that this regular work could help to pay back the bank.

We decided that after finishing my shift for BCal at 7pm, I would come home for a quick shower before driving the lobsters to Luxembourg myself in the rented truck.

The shipment of lobsters would arrive on the evening flight from Newcastle. My friends in the airport cargo department would then clear the paperwork – I always looked after them to thank them for their help.

By that point I had the van ready to go. I would then drive the lobsters the most direct route, through the mountains of Belgium, to Luxembourg where I would wait until they were inspected and accepted, before driving back in the small hours to Amsterdam.

But on arriving at Luxembourg in the small hours of the morning things would go one of two very different ways.

The company importing the seafood to Luxembourg had two partners. One was a gentleman who would fill my flask with fresh coffee before my return and offer me something to eat. The other was a very different kind of man, and it was he who would always claim that too many lobsters were dead on arrival. To prove him wrong, I would open up each of the polystyrene boxes as I pulled them from the back of the truck. There would be between forty to sixty boxes, each containing up to twenty-four lobsters weighing a pound a piece. My diligence made me very popular with the supplier, a Mr Muirhead of Sunderland, and we became friendly. For obvious reasons, he always wanted me to personally deliver the lobsters.

It was a novel way to keep up with the bank payments, but it worked. Although I was on the go the whole time the lobsters solved the problem and within two years we had paid off the entire debt.

As for my cousin, he then did a disappearing act and was nowhere to be seen. In years to come, Patricia and I used to pop into his house off Eaton Terrace, London, and have tea with his wife Vicky, who had been his secretary. She always claimed he was abroad, but Kamel had a uniquely pungent personal odour. It was clear to us that he was hiding in the house and avoiding us. Once, when we were parking, we even saw him looking out of the top floor window.

I always say 'never look back' because if I do the way he treated us still upsets me a little. I believe he had wanted the truck deal to go through successfully, but circumstances outside his control made things go wrong for him.

As to my father's advice, I may have ignored his admonition to never to do business with relatives, but I did take his advice about clearing the bank debt. Today, more than thirty years later and just as he predicted, I am still with my original bank and had paid off the mortgages on my houses before the age of sixty.

Anyway, now you know why I always avoid Lobster Thermidor...

Chapter Sixteen

FRESH MILK
WITHOUT A COW

❧

*People will believe in you if you believe in
yourself – Christen Dominique*

As our airline parts business began to take off in the
mid-1980s, it sometimes felt like we were working
twenty-four hours a day, seven days a week. Yet,
surprisingly, we didn't feel exhausted.

Business is like sport; when it's going well you feel
like you could keep going forever. Watch a losing team
and you see the deflated body language and the sheer
exhaustion on the faces of the defeated players; look
at the winning team and they appear as fresh and
hopeful as the moment they started play. Adrenalin is
the secret weapon of all self-made people.

With all the knowledge I had accumulated over the past twenty-five years, I found it easy to broker and trade aircraft parts. While I was busy making deals, Patricia did all the accounting and administration.

Business was good and soon we had to build extra office space in the back yard.

When we started out in our small cellar, we had a telex machine and we would sit on the cellar stairs near our wine rack to operate it. Telex was the forerunner of the fax machine.

It was clear that we needed more space. When I told my Dutch friend, Pete Damen, he immediately said, "I'll help you build an office." A big strong guy, responsible for refuelling aircraft at the airport, he used to help me on his days off – we called him 'the bodyguard' on account of the disparity in our heights.

So, in the back of our garden, Pete and I built a beautiful brick building with one room for me and one room for Patricia; because we were building on soft, reclaimed land below sea level this needed special 'camel foot' foundations.

And that was the second step. From the cellar we went to the garden.

At this point all we wanted was enough money to pay the mortgage and school fees, and to go on holidays. We wanted a comfortable life.

We learned from the ancient Greeks that flying is a

serious deal that requires high quality tested and certified parts, and my unique selling point was my deep knowledge of the parts I was selling. Being too honest is generally considered bad for business but I turned this assumption on its head.

I was an engineer; I didn't know how to sell ice-cream to Eskimos. So, when the purchasing department of an airline contacted me for a particular component I would engage them in talk about football or the weather before talking about the part. Rather than attempt a quick sell, I would laboriously take them through all the modification details, the part's condition, the name of the workshop that carried out the overhaul, and so on – more information than they could possibly want.

Most of the time they were only interested in the price and the delivery date, and once I gave them that they were happy to place an order having been convinced of the quality of the component on offer.

I worked during the evening while Europe was off duty or asleep, taking orders until midnight which was 3pm Los Angeles time. This meant we were then ready to ship the materials the following morning, before the Europeans started work. It worked very well and the deals flooded in. My bank was very flexible with me and gave me an overdraft facility of more than £100,000, which eased cash flow.

But however busy we were with Fersam and our shifts for British Caledonian, Patricia and I always made a point of having supper at the table with the children. I was very close to Ferdy at this point. When he was exhausted and had homework I used to do his maths or physics for him, being careful to copy his handwriting so the teacher would not know it was not his work.

While we were eating I liked to test my children on their capital cities and to set them little mental arithmetic puzzles.

"At the first bus stop five passengers got on board, at the next bus stop two passengers got on board and three got off, at the next one four passengers got on..." and so on. They would avidly keep a tally on their fingers, but at the very end I wouldn't ask for the number of passengers, I'd surprise them by asking, "So, how many bus stops did the driver make?"

"Oh Daddy, that's cruel," they would wail, secretly delighted that they had been caught out. Then we would go back over the puzzle to work out the answer. It really used to make me laugh, but it also taught them to think laterally and look for opportunity.

This was precisely the attitude of mind that led me to decide to bring fresh milk to an island that had no cows. It was certainly an opportunity, and it definitely required some lateral thinking.

Saint Martin, in the north-eastern Caribbean, is an island with a unique status; the northern half is French and the southern half is Dutch, a fact of geography that dates back to the Treaty of Concordia in 1648. With its brightly painted houses, flamboyant vegetation and turquoise waters it's a beautiful place, but in the mid-1980s fresh milk was unavailable there.

Now there are cows all over the island, some even bask on the beach while tourists take photographs, but back then there was no milk production at all.

Imagine being able to deliver fresh rehydrated milk – now known as reconstituted milk – to a population that had only ever been able to get hold of its UHT alternative? It was so exciting – making milk that goes off like proper milk. For transplanted foreigners living out their days under the hot Caribbean sun, having access to a carton of real milk to pour into their coffee or over their cereal on a daily basis was an idea that was too good to ignore.

Fersam was starting to do well so I decided to buy a 33 per cent share in a company that had really caught my attention. I was keen to do something away from aviation and I didn't believe we could fail.

However, having a hand in running Dominion Foods on Saint Martin proved to be one of the most surreal experiences of my life. What I had not realised at the point when I raised £128,000 for my stake was that the island functioned just like something out of the Pirates of the Caribbean. During the few years I was involved there, things become increasingly lawless and peculiar.

The curious incident of the fresh milk without a cow all started when one of our BCal air hostesses introduced me to her friend Barry P, an expert in evaporation and processing methods. In short, he knew how to turn milk that was close to its expiry date into milk powder. Barry had also discovered that the Caribbean was a spot that did not have much fresh milk, or many cows for that matter.

Putting these two facts together, he had found a small company on the mountainous thirty-four-square mile island of Saint Martin that was willing to rent us their desalination plant. It was the ideal location to manufacture our products.

While most milk processing companies are interested in the drying process, we were going to do things the other way around by mixing the milk powder and butter oil with desalinated seawater and selling the reconstituted result to all the island's supermarkets.

My job was to arrange the shipping to Saint Martin of the vacuum-packed milk powder from Vreugdenhil Dairy Foods, a company in the east of Holland. We also purchased butter oil which is mixed with the powder to make the solution creamy.

After the first few shipments, I visited Saint Martin and was impressed. I watched as the milk powder and the butter oil were homogenised with the desalinated water before being pasteurised and packed in cartons. It was an amazing procedure.

And when I downed the first big glass of our Saint Martin milk it was impossible to tell the difference between real milk and this fresh Caribbean equivalent. The product was sound.

The same could not be said of some of the technical aspects of the factory.

On my first visit to the island I noticed a local boy who had been hired to keep his finger on a switch while production was taking place.

"What's he doing?" I asked our manager, Mr Peters.

"He's keeping his finger on that button," Mr Peters explained.

"Why? What's it for?" I questioned.

It turned out that this boy, whose name was James, was supporting his seven brothers as well as his mother by keeping his finger on the switch. The idea was that it would override the circuit breaker – some idiot had fiddled around with the plant's electrical connection.

I fixed that, but then the poor boy didn't have a job.

I didn't want to pay him to press the button a moment longer than necessary, but neither did I want James to lose out.

"He goes onto production," I told Mr Peters.

James was soon emptying crates of raw material and packing up the cartons of milk ready for the morning delivery. He was so happy that he no longer had to spend his day pressing a switch.

We had bought and imported a gleaming Ford refrigerator truck from Miami and we hired a local driver called Victor. It was Victor's job to collect the milk from the manufacturing plant each morning and deliver it to the twenty-three supermarkets on the island as well as taking cream and milk to the island's restaurants.

All went well for a few weeks, but then I got a call from one of the supermarkets.

"Master," – they always called me master – "The milk is going off before the sell-by date."

Two days later I took a similar call from another of our stockists.

I phoned Barry P, our milk expert.

"What should we do about the fact the milk is going off?" I asked him.

He seemed a bit surprised and suggested that we should turn up the temperature by six degrees

Fahrenheit during the homogenisation process – this is the mechanical method that breaks the fat globules into smaller droplets so that they stay suspended in the milk rather than separating out and floating to the top of the jug.

"You can't increase the temperature any more than that or the milk will boil and form a froth on top," he cautioned.

We did as he had advised, but still the supermarkets told us the milk was not lasting as long as it should.

"Victor, where are you going with the milk?" I asked our driver one day. "Master, I always go straight to the supermarkets," said Victor.

This was good. I had told Victor that when he had a heavy load he should always go to the supermarkets first and only make his deliveries to the restaurants on the way back. The supermarkets needed the longest possible shelf life on the milk but the restaurants would use it immediately.

But because I still couldn't understand why the milk was going off before its sell-by date, I decided to turn private detective and follow Victor. I wanted to see for myself the route he was taking on his daily milk-round.

The following morning, I got up early and by 5am was

waiting in my car in a side turning off the main road half a mile from our factory. On Saint Martin the day is finished by 8am and the locals spend the rest of the day relaxing, so everything is done in the early morning.

After a few minutes, I saw our Ford truck approaching on the main road. I pulled out behind Victor and followed him into the countryside. After half a mile he pulled into some bushes at the side of the road where the locals had their simple wooden houses. I parked up and waited. After a minute the truck appeared from the bushes and drove on again.

Four hundred yards later he pulled over and a boy appeared behind some scrub. The kid opened the back of the truck, jumped in and shut the door.

As Victor moved off so did I. After driving another couple of hundred metres the same thing happened again. To cut a long story short, Victor did this at least a dozen times until he reached a school.

At that point he pulled over and I watched fifteen children get out of the back of my refrigerated vehicle.

I couldn't believe it. Victor was using our milk truck as a school bus.

"Victor, where the fuck is the milk?" I said when I accosted him at the driver's window.

"Oh master, I left it near the factory. It's alright master," he insisted.

"Take me there now," I instructed.

Sure enough the milk was sitting on a bit of land in the sunshine, warming all the way through.

I had no choice but to fire him.

"Sorry master," he pleaded. "I have a wife here, I have a wife in Anguilla, and I have a wife in Saint Thomas. I have to look after them all."

He had lied to me so there was no second chance; you have to be able to trust the people you work with.

And there was yet another area that had been causing concern; the water bill.

We had a well at the desalination plant but when it was dry we had to buy in metered water. Water in Saint Martin is very expensive, but we were spending something like £600 on water every month. It was a horrendous amount of money.

And there was a further problem. Why was the well always running dry?

"It's rained heavily," I said to Mr Peters. "Why the hell isn't the well full?"

The island of Saint Martin has a tropical monsoon climate. The total yearly rainfall is half as much again as the UK. In fact, it rains more days of the year in Saint Martin it does in Britain.

Immediately, I set about investigating the cause.

I followed the plumbing and saw that the plumber

had set things up in the wrong direction. Rather than the water in the well flowing into the milk plant, we were paying to fill the well with desalinated water. It took me a couple of days to discover the reason why.

After a few days of scratching my head, I decided to get to the plant early. I arrived at 4am and was surprised to see a water bowser parked up next to the main entrance. I saluted the men who were next to it and they waved back, thinking I was one of the lads. I stood some distance away and watched them at work.

What they were doing defied belief. They were pumping water from the well and filling the water truck. They then drove away. This went on for the next few days. It didn't take long to discover that they were selling this water to their clients who needed water for their swimming pools.

We fired the responsible culprits and sorted out the plumbing. From that point on we never needed to buy another drop of water because the well was always full.

Within a year we were manufacturing eleven different products – including Patricia's favourite chocolate milk – and making a real success of it. We were producing double cream and chocolate as well as orange and apple juices from concentrates. People were buying, it was a good business and were able to supply our third partner with fresh water for his hotel.

Meanwhile, this was a testing time in aviation. All the airlines were making a loss. There wasn't a direct risk to me of being laid off because there is always a shortage of qualified engineers; the real risk was the threat of the company closing down. There was a lot of talk at that time of airlines going bankrupt and rumours were rife that the Scandinavian airline SAS wanted to buy British Caledonian.

While all this was rumbling on I knew that getting Fersam as well-established as I could while I was still young was crucial.

For the next couple of years, I spent all my leave in the Caribbean in the milk plant. I used to go twice, sometimes three times a year, via Puerto Rico, and on one occasion I took Patricia and Julian, convinced that the warm dry air would help my son's asthma. It did.

When Julian was five we took him to Egypt to see the pyramids, and to meet his Egyptian family. It was my first and last time on a camel. Patricia wanted Julian to ride so I hired two camels, one for me and one for Julian. But Patricia insisted that Julian was too young to ride a camel on his own.

"I will guard him with my eyes, Sir," insisted the guide.

This was not enough for Patricia. Apparently only I

could protect our son. I knew better than to argue so I instructed the guide to bring Julian to my camel and sit him on the howdah with me. Unfortunately, it turned out that my camel was sick and had the runs. We should have ridden on Julian's camel who was quite well thank you, and walked just behind us.

Everything was running well at the milk plant until my partner in Dominion Foods, Barry P, hit a marital minefield when his wife Sheila discovered the existence of his mistress, Mary. Sheila left the Caribbean declaring she would never come back and Barry stopped spending so much time on the island.

Things began to fall apart. We started to go into the red and we had creditors. It didn't make sense, we were supplying the milk to the supermarkets – why weren't they paying?

Mr Peters was employed as the manager of Dominion Foods but appeared to have no interest in what was happening.

I flew out to Saint Martin to find out what was going on. After another fourteen-hour flight I arrived. The plant was in disarray. There were no returns or profits shown in any the books. And the milk powder and butter oil I was sending were being stolen.

I used to ship twenty bags of milk powder and seven bags of butter oil at a time, but when I looked at the paperwork from the ship, twenty bags had become fifteen, and the butter oil had reduced to five.

"Mr Peters, what is going on?" I demanded.

"No Sir, you only send me fifteen bags," he insisted.

I showed him the dispatch note, but it was pointless. It was brazen piracy and I was sure Peters was in it up to his neck, but I couldn't fire him because he was the nephew of Claude Wathey, the leader of the government on the Dutch side of the island. Business would become impossible if I got rid of Mr Peters. Under Wathey's administration, Saint Martin was transforming from a neglected colonial backwater into a thriving tourist destination with one of the highest per capita incomes in the region. There were some serious deals being cut.

I demanded to know why the supermarkets had stopped paying.

"Oh no sir, I did ring them," said Peters, squirming.

Anyway, I decided to take the car and get James to show me where all the supermarkets were.

We arrived at the first one and we went inside holding the paperwork.

"I'm here from Dominion Foods, and by the way you owe us £350," I said.

"Yes sir," said the manager. "I have a cheque here but nobody came to collect it."

He handed it over. It was the same story at every

one of the twenty-three supermarkets we visited that morning. I collected so much money, it was unbelievable.

I took it down to the bank and wiped out our overdraft.

Then I went back to the manufacturing plant.

"Mr Peters, your priority is to collect the money," I said.

"Yes sir, but I didn't have time."

"You didn't have time," I spluttered. "Why? What do you do after 7am when you've stopped production?"

"I have to go home for breakfast," he explained.

"Then what happens?" I demanded.

He didn't have an answer for that because he was another big arsehole. The place was crawling with these pirates. Captain Jack Sparrow would have fitted right in.

That night we met a Frenchman in the bar. "You know, to be honest, if you want a business to work on Saint Martin you have to be here twenty-four-seven. Otherwise, close your eyes and you'll get robbed," he said. "The only way to make it work here is to pick up every cheque yourself."

We realised we had to get out. Our other partner, a hotelier named Manuel, wanted to buy us out, but Barry P blocked it because it would have given his rival a controlling stake.

So to this day we are still the shareholders of Dominion Foods, which I understand is still running with a continuous deficit, with nothing to show in return for our investment. It was a good business until Barry P spoiled it all, but we vowed never to go back there because of the pirates. It was a strange place, Saint Martin.

I felt really disappointed, but I had learned yet another lesson; Never go into business with someone else – one's wife excluded, of course. It's just as my father always said; "If you want to do a job properly, do it yourself."

The Dominion Foods debacle showed us that we should focus on what we knew; aircraft parts. After all the challenges we had faced we had finally recognised that we should concentrate on that. And it was a good thing too, because everything was about to change.

Chapter Seventeen

ROTABLES AND EXPENDABLES

❧

A man begins cutting his wisdom teeth
the first time he bites off more than he
can chew – Herb Caen

In 1986, British Caledonian reported losses of £25 million following the disappearance of £6 million worth of South American business after the Falklands War. The war, which lasted just two months, one week and five days, may have been short-lived, but the knock-on effects were significant. Also contributing to the airline's losses was the United States bombing of Libya on 15th April 1986, which had closed off BCal's lucrative route to Libya. The attack had been carried out by the United States in retaliation for the Berlin discotheque bombing.

Arnold came to see me, and he was very frank.

The company was in serious financial trouble.

Things had become so parlous that the airline was in danger of not being able to pay its salaries.

With 7,000 employees, BCal needed to find £1 million every month just to pay the staff.

Consequently, the company was thinking creatively about how to come up with the money and had put Arnold in charge of a programme to generate some of the money by selling spare material owned by the airline.

And he needed my help.

In short, I was being asked to sell off any spare aircraft parts in order to pay the salaries of my co-workers.

Arnold knew I had been dabbling privately in the sale of light aviation items, things such as nuts, bolts, brackets and fixings – these things are known as expendables or consumables because they cannot be repaired and they are thrown away at the end of their working life. I'd also sold a few cargo equipment pallets, which are used to ship freight in aircraft.

None of this was rocket science.

Now he was asking me to concentrate on selling higher value rotables to make urgently needed cash for the company. A rotable is a component that carries a serial number and is usually tracked on an airline's database. It is also a part that can be rebuilt or overhauled and put back in stock to use again – things such as hydraulics, fuel controls, and engine and landing gear equipment. These are the parts that, if they fail, might give the pilots a bad day. So care is taken when they're built, calibrated and installed.

I knew these parts intimately of course, but selling them – and knowing their worth on the open market – well, that was an entirely new and unfamiliar world to me.

The price of aircraft parts is never disclosed to engineers because there is a risk that it might affect one's judgement, so I was going to have to make contact with British Caledonian's purchasing department.

Before he left, Arnold looked me in the eye. "Sell the parts, keep just enough to cover your expenses, and pay back the rest, lad. Okay?" So that's exactly what I did. And I sold quite a bit.

It turned out to be easy to sell the parts because whatever the given value in sterling for an item, I was allowed to sell it for the same number of dollars. This meant the customers were getting a great deal for just 60 per cent of the true value. But more importantly I was able to generate a lot of money for the company.

And there was another advantage to this new role. On company time, I was learning the ropes about selling serious bits of aviation kit. Not only that, but I was doing so with the kind support and guidance of my colleagues in BCal's purchasing department who enlightened me regarding pricing and availability.

I remembered everything they told me.

This was to prove very useful because I was ambitious. My experience generating money for BCal gave me increasing confidence to sell the larger, more valuable components. And I was lucky because, thanks again to Arnold, I had the luxury of time.

The previous year Arnold had sent another engineer to work alongside me in Amsterdam, handling the day-to-day business of turning around our aircraft. This engineer and I got on well and he would call me if ever he needed to consult on a problem. I had the supervisory role, but he was very efficient and because of that I gradually stepped up the private business. It was, thanks to Arnold, a very comfortable arrangement which gave me the spare time to go flat out with Fersam.

I rented a warehouse in Lijndendijk and signed a consignment deal with Casco Ltd in West Sussex, an established supplier to large international airlines and distributors.

I didn't have time to sell the nuts and bolts – brackets for £100, or a little flange or a bag of washers for a few pence. Instead, I would buy the whole lot as

NAZIE A. EL MASRY

a job lot and while I concentrated on selling the high-value items, I consigned the rest to Casco for a percentage of the sale.

This alone gave us a regular monthly income that was coming in without any trouble whatsoever.

I felt confident that whatever happened to BCal, Patricia and I were developing a lucrative sideline of our own.

And, as it turned out, it wouldn't be long before I would see Arnold again.

Maggie Thatcher hated the idea of a British airline being owned by foreigners, but it was clear that something had to happen to save British Caledonian. The airline was at serious risk of collapse. The salaries were still being paid but we were running out of material to sell.

As if the other international geopolitical problems the airline had already faced were not enough, the Chernobyl disaster in April 1986 led to a huge number of cancelled transatlantic bookings and there were also problems with the West African routes due to crushing debt in Nigeria.

British Caledonian began looking in earnest for a merger partner.

SAS had entered the talks but Prime Minister Thatcher was having none of it. She got in touch with

Lord King, the chairman of British Airways, and her favourite businessman who had transformed an inefficient, nationalised company into one of the most successful privatised airlines of recent times.

"Don't let it go," she urged him. "Go and buy Caledonian regardless of the price."

In the end, BA made a take-it-or-leave-it deal worth more than SAS's offer and my 1800 shares in British Caledonian which had been worth £1 each were suddenly worth £10.15 apiece. I sold them immediately.

The merger in December 1987 gave British Airways control of British Caledonian and in so doing created a carrier large enough to compete with the United States' giant air corporations. The £237 million deal was called 'the biggest shake-up in the airline industry for twenty years'.

It was also a turning point in our household because it led to Patricia's decision to take redundancy and a golden handshake, rather than stay on in the newly enlarged company.

Patricia had been offered the chance to become a supervisor in Amsterdam for British Airways, as we were now known, but this would have meant displacing a very good supervisor named Jack. Being ground staff in Schiphol she knew all the BA staff and wasn't prepared to do this.

Coupled with this, Fersam was taking more of our time and Patricia had also been helping our friend Robbie set up a bucket shop business – a travel agency that specialised in providing cheap air tickets – which was currently lurching from one crisis to another.

But most importantly there was Julian to consider. Now aged five, he was still affected by asthma and Patricia wanted to spend more time with our son. Working from home meant she could still feel connected to the aviation industry and closer to her boy at the same time. Ultimately, taking redundancy proved to be the best of both worlds and Patricia was happy.

As for me, Arnold prized me as an engineer and did not want to lose me. But having worked for him for the best part of twenty-five years he had also become my mentor. Between them, Arnold Sheead and Uncle Youssef had guided and supported me through so much.

"Go commercial, lad". These were the life-changing words that Arnold had uttered in his gruff northern tones when we met up for a meal while the merger was being mooted. "You got no place here. If you go commercial, lad, you'll do a lot better," he insisted, adding bluntly, "With your background you'll never be the engineering director of British Airways."

Arnold himself was 100 per cent devoted to the airline and never ran his own business. He was chief engineer and then he became engineering director of British Caledonian, before becoming engineering director of BA at Gatwick, but he recognised that I was an entrepreneur; a different kind of man. He was also being pragmatic about my Egyptian heritage.

Arnold gave me my first job and, eventually, he told me when it was time to leave because he saw I had potential and, I like to believe, because he cared about me.

I had worked for him for quarter of a century, from when I was a youngster to when I was an old boy. It was quite a wrench, but I knew it was the right thing for me to do. I longed to work for myself and to have the time to devote solely to building up my own aircraft parts business.

I had been based in Amsterdam for a very long time and I got on well with the majority of the staff working at Schiphol. I'd known the BA guys there even well before the merger. All the engineers help each other overseas, regardless of airline. We even used to borrow material from one another. The Lufthansa and BA boys would help me and I would help them. We had to do it quickly and we had to do it 'hush-hush', because it was not supposed to happen. You would do the tests and give back the parts. There was always a spirit of cooperation between engineers, regardless of airline and regardless of company policy.

So when I was asked by Barry Foster, BA's SMM (Station Maintenance Manager) to stay on with British Airways for a year or so to ensure continuity following the merger I did not mind too much. As a matter of routine I was sent on courses to prepare me to work on new aircraft. I took part in these training sessions but had made up my mind 100 per cent to go.

Understandably, they did not want to lose an extremely experienced senior engineer and seemed to think a change of scene might make me change my mind. They offered to send me to Milan. I refused. They invited me to go to Madrid. I said no.

I was told that I would have twelve engineers working for me in Milan; twenty-four in Madrid.

"No, I don't want to work for anybody, I'm going to work for myself," I insisted. It's easier to get a 747 to do a barrel roll on one engine than it is to get me to change my mind when I've made a decision.

And this was a resolution about which I was entirely certain.

I had tasted freedom, Fersam was doing well and I was already semi-established thanks to recent experiences. I knew this was the right way forward. I'd had a hell of a job keeping up with two masters and the certainty of certainty was a delightful feeling.

I had a great deal to thank Arnold for.

Whenever he had come to Amsterdam on work-related matters we would always go out for dinner and talk about this and that. I always used to find a good restaurant and I would offer to pay, but at the final moment Arnold would always say, "No! You work for me. I'm going to pay the fucking bill."

At last, it was my turn to pay.

Arnold and I continued to stay in touch. After his retirement he and his wife went to Australia to visit her sister, who lived there. Sadly, he later had a series of strokes. I was lucky to have known him. One could not have had a better boss.

Chapter Eighteen

A HOUSE WITH TWO ENTRANCES

❧

There is no elevator to success, you have to take the stairs – Zig Ziglar

My money has always said two words; "Hi" and "'bye". It comes in and I spend it immediately, and I still do that now. I'm driven to spontaneity by my impulsive nature.

When I took early retirement from British Airways in 1988 at the age of forty-five, I was given a very handsome cheque for five figures. Immediately, I used it to buy a CSD (Constant Speed Drive); a mechanical gearbox that helps to start an aircraft jet engine and generate the electricity that it needs to run smoothly.

Not your average indulgence, but something I knew

With my colleague and friends, Robbie B *(left)* and Hans H *(right)*. Hans was working for me by then and looking after his wife and our colleague Cindy, who had MS.

The first Dutch warehouse we owned, a former butcher's storage facility.

In 1999, we bought a two-acre commercial property in Holland and named it Julian's Farm, after our son.

I had this desk for twenty years. By Friday afternoon I had normally tidied it and was ready to start a new chapter. I used the microfiche machine to study aircraft parts numbers in the illustrated parts catalogues.

My lovely daughter Samantha at the age of 24, shortly after she graduated. I had put on a bit of weight due to good living and the fact I had recently given up sport.

With my oldest friend Angus Whiteside *(left)*, stepson of my mentor
Dougie Goldstein - at Samantha's wedding in 2000.

With my dear friend Ernst Grossman *(left)*, a former Lufthansa senior
engineer. We go back more than three decades to our time in Amsterdam
and elsewhere in Europe. We also met in the US and had a good time.
Today, he is one of my most trusted business advisors.

I always like to try anything new. This was taken in 2001 outside the warehouse at Julian's Farm.

Patricia and me celebrating in 2005: We are always celebrating.

My cousin Ezzat who was the witness to my marriage to Patricia in 1977. He lived in Baltimore with his wife, Nadia. This photo was taken when they visited us in Holland in 2006, eight years before he died.

We had just acquired this SAS Boeing 737-400 for tear down. The year was 2014 and the start of a new direction for the company.

My wonderful grandchildren: *(Left to right)* Ruben, Kate, Thomas, and Oliver. Samantha's boys loved spending time with their younger cousins at Julian's wedding in 2015.

A happy family: Our son Julian with his wife Sharon and their children, Oliver, four, and Kate, two, on their wedding day at the International Golf Club in Amsterdam.

One of my favourite photographs: It was Nana and Grandad's job to keep little Kate and Oliver out of mischief. Kate was only two and had borrowed Patricia's hat. My daughter-in-law's elegant grandmother Hetty, who remarkably was in her late eighties, is also seated next to me *(left)*.

I was proud to witness the marriage of my son Julian.

(Left to right) My best friend Robbie B, Julian, and me: I am godfather to Robbie and Chencho's daughter Daniella.

Robbie B *(right)* is my best friend and Julian's godfather. Robbie and I met at British Caledonian in Amsterdam in 1973 and have been close ever since.

Julian and me in our matching grey suits with TDA's sales team after manning our stand at the Maintenance, Repair and Overhaul (MRO) exhibition in Amsterdam. Such trade fairs for the aeronautical maintenance industry are held internationally several times a year.

We're local. All over the world: TDA's stand at the MRO exhibition in Miami, Florida. Julian and I are both seated. The sales guys are answering questions from potential new clients – the maintenance and repair organisations who require reliable parts' suppliers, such as TDA.

Our new warehouse facility at TDA's Amsterdam HQ near Schiphol airport which we bought in March 2016. It's hard to believe we had started our business 34 years earlier in a cellar with an old telex machine.

My daughter Samantha *(left)* and Patricia *(right)* in the warehouse at Julian's Farm, Holland: I never wanted to keep spares but now I've got four warehouses, on three continents, covering around 400,000 square feet.

Our London HQ in Slinfold, West Sussex; this former BASF warehouse is now full of parts ready to supply aircraft at Gatwick, Heathrow and beyond.

Our HQ in Miami, Florida; there is another warehouse behind this office. We have a worldwide presence so we can supply parts internationally within hours.

The view from our house in Spain: I have enjoyed commissioning the building of houses since taking semi-retirement from TDA. © Jane Warren

Our house in Altea on the Costa Blanca was designed by the late Spanish architect Carlos Gilardi, following my brief for a house with curves. He used a photograph of it on his company Christmas card in 2015, the year after it was completed. © Jane Warren

My garage in Spain is cut into the hillside beneath our home. Julian gave me the personalised number plate on my Bentley Flying Spur for my 70th birthday present in 2013. © Jane Warren

I appreciate it when things are engineered with precision, including the kitchen at our house on the Costa Blanca. © Jane Warren

Patricia and I spend the autumn and winter months of the year in Altea, Spain. This photograph was taken at Saltea, one of our favourite restaurants.

Together with my son Julian: we have always had a
very close relationship.

A recent photograph of me, taken this year. I will be 75 on 3rd January 2018, but I still feel as if I am in my twenties or thirties.

I could buy at a good price and sell for an even better one.

It turned out to be a wise investment.

Together with Patricia's redundancy money we were now in a position to buy a second house in Badhoevedorp.

Dr Sabel had been a well-known doctor in the city and had a house with an attached surgery. His son Paul happened to be my GP. When Patricia and I discovered that the house belonging to our GP's late father had been on the market for two years we decided to buy it because it was built on the corner of two residential streets.

The doorway at Amersfoordtlaan 30 led to his surgery and the doorway at Roerdompstraat 30 around the corner, led to his private residence. I got my estate agent involved to negotiate the price and he came up with a figure that was acceptable to my GP and his siblings.

For an ambitious couple working from home the layout was perfect for us. In one move we had acquired both a residential and a business address.

We set about renovating the house to our taste with money left over from Patricia's redundancy cheque and my golden handshake.

This generated quite a bit of interest locally. People kept on saying, "Oh you bought the house of the doctor, we were thinking of buying it" or "I had my husband investigate it and he wanted to buy it."

Suddenly everyone had wanted to buy it. It had been empty for two years and nobody had even looked at it. So as soon as we bought it was all "we wanted to buy it".

It turned out there was also quite a bit of gossip about the identity of the new owners of Dr Sabel's house, as you would expect in a small town. Owners, it must be said, who were clearly spending a small fortune on extensive renovations before setting foot inside.

We found this out when Patricia went to the local cheese shop a minute's walk down Amersfoordtlaan. We were also lucky to have a bakery and greengrocer a short walk from the house, but the cheese shop we knew well because we had already been customers for a while.

Patricia was queuing for her turn to choose delicious cheeses for our table that night when she overheard the two old ladies in front of her gossiping.

"You know those people who have bought Dr Sabel's house?" said one.

"Oh yes," said the other, eagerly.

"Well, it turns out that they are arms dealers."

"Oh my goodness, I can't believe it," said her friend.

"Do you really think so, Dames?" said Leo Schmidt, the owner of the cheese shop – he clearly knew his gossiping customer by name.

"Yes, that's the truth. Arms dealers, Leo. Arms dealers," insisted Dames, with a knowing nod of her head.

With a large smile spreading over his face, Mr Schmidt allowed them to continue speculating as he wrapped up their purchases.

"Well, ladies," he said when he was done. "That will be fifteen guilders and forty-eight cents please. And while you are here I'd like to introduce you to Mrs El Masry. She and her husband have just bought Dr Sabel's house."

Well, the looks on their faces as they turned to look at Patricia waiting in the queue behind them were apparently indescribable.

They couldn't get out of there fast enough; one of them even left her shopping bag behind.

Naturally, Patricia and Mr Schmidt found the whole incident highly amusing.

After a few months' work, the house was ready and we moved in.

The builders had done a fine job and it was wonderful to have generous office space.

I never needed to travel to work. At 8.55am I would leave the breakfast table and step into my office ready for the busy day ahead.

Inevitably, after we had moved in there were still

things to do to get the house just as we wanted it. Although tools still weren't my forte I didn't think it could be particularly hard to hang pictures. Emboldened by my success, I decided to tackle the job of drilling holes for some shelf fixings in the hall outside Julian's bedroom.

"No need to get a builder in," I thought confidently, "When you can do it yourself."

I got to work with my ten-inch masonry drill bit and then I heard Julian talking to me over the noise of the drilling.

"Hello Daddy," he said.

I turned off the drill.

"Hello Julian, how are you?"

"I can see you Daddy!" he exclaimed.

"Where are you Julian?" I asked

And then I noticed that he had run back into his bedroom and was peering at me through the hole I had just drilled straight through the wall.

Over the next few years the business grew fast and everything snowballed. It turned out I had a real knack as a trader selling specialist aviation parts. From the first few sentences of a new enquiry I found I could sense just how interested in a component a customer was, as well as how much I was likely to be able to squeeze out of them. This instinct was further refined with practice.

And every deal I did was underscored by my inner alarm bell, by my desire to be honest with myself and by my inability to relax if I had overlooked something. For example, if I made an agreement with a client and realised later that I had neglected to tell them something important, I found literally that I could not rest until I had contacted them and cleared it up.

On one occasion I sold an engine to Delta Airlines, who are based in Atlanta, Georgia, from KLM, the Royal Dutch Airlines. Letters of credit were ready to go on both sides, but something was niggling me.

The engine had come off an Airbus 310, but Delta were planning to fit it into a Boeing 767-200 owned by FedEx, who would operate the plane. That really bothered me because I knew there must be a difference in the configurations of things like the electrical connections and panels that would allow it to be mounted on the new aircraft. The worst case scenario was that we would have to pay for the alterations.

I did not rest until I contacted Delta's quality assurance people. A day later I received a message that although there were indeed some differences they were prepared to meet the costs of reconfiguration. Boy, was I relieved, and so was my inner alarm clock.

The hard work was always there, but as one gets older and wiser you learn more and make fewer mistakes, as in any business. One of the major pitfalls in this business is the risk of buying bogus parts. They are very common in our industry because of the massive cost of the material. Every now and then you come across parts that have been copied, or components that have been manufactured illegally, and sometimes the historical records of the part are questionable – the equivalent in aviation terms to turning back a car's milometer.

We didn't get a lot of bogus parts because having been an aeronautical engineer for twenty-five years I was very familiar with the equipment and could usually sniff one out a mile away. When you have handled real parts, the bogus ones are immediately apparent; sometimes from the colour of the primer used or from the way the electrical unions are attached to the body.

My focus was on engine parts, and because of my knowledge in this area I only ended up buying a few things which had to go into the dustbin. But even with the mistakes, there is usually value in the raw material.

However, as our business grew so did the problem with our name.

Chapter Nineteen

TOUCHDOWN

∞

Much of the success of life depends upon keeping one's mind open to opportunity and seizing it when it comes – Alice Foote MacDougall

Having spontaneously named the company after the first three letters of my two eldest children's names, I had discovered that 'Fersam' did not travel very well by word of mouth. In fact, it seemed prone to a corporate version of Chinese whispers.

Increasingly, people who had heard about our reputation were ringing me up and calling us 'Fersham' or 'Firstham' and one day someone even asked why we had decided to call ourselves 'First Hand' given that we traded in second hand parts.

At the end of 1989 I flew to America. When I landed

at San Antonio airport in Texas, I saw a massive banner advertisement for the final of the Super Bowl on the road outside the terminal. In large letters, next to details of the annual championship game of the National Football League, was the word 'Touchdown'.

I wasn't interested in American football, but in a flash of inspiration I decided to rename the aviation parts business Touchdown Components (later Touchdown Aviation) because I liked the play on words. We kept Fersam for our various dealings in property.

Nowadays there are several companies, petrol stations and even corner shops calling themselves Touchdown, so in time we decided to simplify things further and became TDA.

Soon we were in a position to rent warehouse space and take on staff.

Our first employee was Cindy, a former member of BCal's ground staff at London Gatwick who had been expatriated with her husband Hans to Hong Kong.

During our Schiphol days there had been four of us working for British Caledonian in Amsterdam. I was the Station Engineer; Patricia was on the ticket desk; Robbie B was the Station Manager and Hans H was Robbie's assistant and Patricia's boss at the airport. We were all the best of friends and had a lot of fun together. It was during those years, in the 1980s, that

Robbie and his wife Chencho, a Philippine dancer, had given me the marijuana seeds which had caused us all so much amusement.

Cindy was married to Hans, so we knew her well also. After I left BA these dear friends were posted by the airline to Hong Kong, but one day when Cindy was out walking she tripped and fell. She thought it was due to a loose paving slab but then it happened again, and it turned out she had MS (multiple sclerosis). Shortly after this Cindy and Hans returned to Amsterdam; unfortunately, he was then made redundant.

I hired Cindy as my secretary, aware that she had MS and was facing the inevitable deterioration caused by this degenerative neurological disorder. I was glad to help her. She answered the phone and handled the mail. She wasn't very good at actually typing but she was a pleasant person and she had a friendly telephone manner.

She worked for us for six or seven years until her MS had taken her to a point where she could barely move. Initially it wasn't too bad, but her condition steadily deteriorated.

Her husband Hans started working for me in 1988 when Cindy no longer could. He was my PR man who would go and promote the company with our suppliers and customers, as well as looking after all the admin

— aircraft parts always require a lot of paperwork due to the need for certification and a history, and so on. He proved to be very good at all that.

In 1993, we were ready to move to a larger warehouse in the centre of Badhoevedorp. It was the first we owned. At just over 5,000 square feet it was more than enough for our operations. It had been home to Arie van de Raa, a family butchers, until the owner was given a subsidy to move to a new warehouse on reclaimed land a few miles away.

The butcher was more than happy to get rid of his old place and for us it was ideal as it was within walking distance of our house. I got a mortgage and together with the help of some friends we divided the warehouse into serviceable and unserviceable parts. The warehouse came complete with a lot of shelving which was handy for all these materials.

And we certainly needed those shelves the following year when KLM decided to sell off the contents of an entire hanger which they wanted to rebuild. Mr Z, KLM's parts sales manager, needed to clear the lot.

As the inventory was too much for me I made a deal with a fellow I knew who dealt in scrap materials. Cock van B was his name, but no Rip van Winkle was he. With alacrity, he immediately set about negotiating for the contents of hanger No. 10 with Mr Z.

The deal was that he would take the scrap and I

would hang on to the avionics and actuators and all the other things I knew about. The deal was concluded speedily and was a very exciting moment for me. I was now beginning to sell plum components to big aircraft parts dealers, and about to make a lot of contacts along the way.

But my biggest problem was cash flow. I needed to move the stuff and fast. I had been taught by one of my business mentors, Dougie Goldstein, that the secret ingredient to a good deal is the initial purchase price. "Buy right," he would say, "And if you buy cheap enough you can always offload the parts quickly."

The basic thing was to ensure that you always gave yourself enough room to make a modest profit.

I started out by selling to dealers. The key was not to be too greedy as a means to ensure that the stuff did not sit around for too long. This made the dealers happy because they were able to buy cheap from us; then they would then really sting the airline.

That was another of Dougie Goldstein's great pieces of advice. "You mustn't be killing your vendors all the time, you really have to know how to pacify them".

The first thing I would do on buying new stock was to get rid of the 'sugar lumps'. These are the choice, high-value items which give the biggest return; things such as landing gear and instrumentation.

I made my first call to a well-known aviation parts

dealer in California named Mike S, with whom I'd been dealing for a few years with smaller bits and pieces.

"Hey Magnum, would you like to buy some autothrottle computers?" (These are devices that allow a pilot to control the power setting of an aircraft's engines.)

"Oh hi, Naz," he said in his American twang. "Yeah, I'd very much like 'em," he enthused. And I sold them to him for big money. Then I sold the anti-skid control boxes and the generators, and all the other sugar lumps, for equally big money.

Soon I had a reputation for selling top quality components at very low prices. I was happy with my low profit margin as I also had very low overheads. In time, it got to the point that as soon as a dealer was looking for KLM parts they would contact me. I lived very close to the airport so, as you can imagine, I was in and out all the time looking for surplus material to buy.

Incidentally, the reason I call Mike 'Magnum' goes back to the day I first met him in California. Every few months I used to travel to the United States to generate business. Mike used to work for a large company called Aviation Sales Corp, and I used to sell him a lot of material, so one day we arranged to meet and have breakfast together before I went to meet my other clients – he started work at 5am every morning.

I asked how I would recognise him at Los Angeles airport.

"Oh that's easy, Naz. I look like Magnum, PI."

"Great," I said. A few days later as I stepped into the arrivals hall I was looking for a tall, rangy Tom Selleck lookalike.

I couldn't see him anywhere. The only person I could see was short, with a big belly and a pointed bald head, but he did have Tom Selleck's distinctive bushy moustache. Other than that, Mike didn't look a bit like the American actor. It really made me laugh and we struck up a working relationship that lasted years.

As business grew, the funds were accumulating and soon I had the spare cash to renovate our home, the former doctor's surgery. I had big plans. First I built an extension on the ground floor behind the building to expand our offices. Then I built an electric roof in automated sections over the patio and installed an in-ground Jacuzzi. I also installed a big Jacuzzi into the master bedroom upstairs. My background as an engineer is all about precision and everything was done to a very high specification.

All this was to prove a very good investment because it turned out that we would not be living there very much longer.

In 1995 we decided to invest some of our profits in

making a deposit on a rental property. Frisolaan 10 was one of the biggest houses in Badhoevedorp with a footprint of 18,000 square feet, including a 500 square foot dining room. It was vast. We planned to rent it out to cover our mortgages and ease cash flow while we accumulated more funds to renovate the house, which was in dire need of a face-lift as it was dominated by dark wood everywhere you looked.

The house was being sold by Theo Brenninkmeyer, the second of the three reclusive German brothers who co-own the department store chain C&A named after their ancestors, the founder brothers Clemens and August – hence C&A – who established it in 1841.

It took Theo more than an hour to explain all the ins and outs of that house to me. Not only did it have a sauna and a Jacuzzi, it had an air conditioning system to stop the windows by the indoor pool from steaming up with condensation.

It also had four large bedrooms with attached bathrooms, several reception rooms, a large kitchen with a breakfast area, an additional sitting room by the pool, and a vast basement with its own private access. We thought this would be ideal for thirteen-year-old Julian in years to come as it could easily be converted into a self-contained bachelor pad.

Our offer was accepted, and Patricia and I set about

finding a tenant. A few weeks went by before our agent phoned to say he thought he had found the ideal candidate. Mr A worked for the European arm of the Japanese global investment bank, Nomura. Apparently this Japanese gentleman liked the house just as it was, even before any renovations.

Two days later Mr A called me and asked if we could meet.

"I love the house but there is a problem, Mr El Masry," he explained carefully. "I am the European president of Nomura bank. The president and vice president of the bank are based in Tokyo. The problem is that neither of them have an indoor pool there. In Japanese culture it is a matter of status. It would be considered offensive for me to rent such a villa with an indoor pool given this, and sadly for that reason I am afraid I cannot rent Frisolaan."

One always has to seize opportunity. He was a lovely man and an ideal tenant and I didn't want him to get away.

"Would you like to rent my other house?" I found myself saying. "We've just finished renovating it. It has a Jacuzzi but no pool."

I went home and found Patricia reading a book in the garden.

"Do you want the good news or the bad news?" I asked her.

"The good news, Nazie," she said.

"We rented the house!"

"I know that, Nazie; what is the bad news," she asked.

"The bad news is that we rented *this* house and we have ten days to move out."

Patricia went absolutely ballistic.

Two weeks later, we watched as two large trucks full of our possessions arrived at Frisolaan from our previous home less than a mile away. The removal company were professionals. Do you know, they even wrapped an ashtray with ash in it, all taped up and labelled with the contents.

All went well with Mr A's tenancy until he moved out in 1999. However, when the time came to check the property over I found a large hole in the Jacuzzi which had caused the water level to drop. I got hold of my insurance guy and asked him to come and assess the damage.

"What the hell do you think this hole is?" I asked him.

"Sir, for forty years I have been an insurance assessor and I've never seen a lightning strike in water like this. I'm glad nobody was in here; they would have been roasted alive," he said, marvelling at the idea.

I phoned Mr A. "There's been a lightning strike in the Jacuzzi," I said.

"Yes," he said, "My wife and I were enjoying the Jacuzzi together when a big storm began. We decided to go inside the house but we forgot to close the retracting roof. We were so lucky; we had only just gone inside the house when there was an explosion outside."

I know Japanese couples like to spend time together in Jacuzzis, so I pointed out that I had installed a large one upstairs as well.

"Ah, but you see my wife, she likes the fresh air," he began.

"I don't want to know," I laughed. "I'm just glad you weren't busy in the Jacuzzi when the lightning struck."

During his tenancy we had been occupied with the renovations at Frisolaan. After painting the entire interior white, which made a huge different to the sense of space in the house, we enclosed the centre patio. This became a dining room with a bar area; the epicentre of our home. In the basement we created a sitting room, bedroom and another bar unit for Julian to entertain his friends; his apartment also had its own private exit. Finally, we invested in a coffee machine and a wine cellar to keep my lovely wine collection at a constant temperature.

Hans stayed with us loyally for twenty-two years and

continued to care for Cindy at home for as long as he could. He would bathe her and do her laundry, and lift her when she could no longer move. Eventually he had to accept that she needed to move to a full-time care facility and once she was there he visited her every single day.

We would have a beer together at 5.30pm and at 6pm, on the dot, he would leave to visit Cindy. Apparently, she used to tell him off if he was late. The staff at the home would offer to do her laundry and Cindy would explain, "No, Hans has to do it." It was the same story with friends. Once when we went to visit her, we offered to dispose of a rubbish bag propped against the wall in her room and awaiting collection. "No, Hans will take it." On that occasion I also offered to help her change position because she looked uncomfortable. "Oh no," she explained carefully. "Hans will do it when he arrives." I felt very sorry for them both.

The tragedy was that he had become so engrossed in looking after Cindy that Hans had become rather unwell.

One Friday night, after our regular after-work beer, he arrived home and had a massive stroke in his kitchen. There was nobody there to help him and he was not discovered by a neighbour until the following day. It was such a shock to all of us.

Without Hans, Cindy had nothing to live for and she died a few months later.

Hans was a great loss to the company. He had been with us through all the changes that the years had brought, and his photo is still hanging in our office.

These developments included the beginning of our direct dealings with airlines themselves. I had graduated now from dealing solely with aviation parts dealers and had built up my contacts with KLM, Lufthansa, Philippine Airlines and SAS – the Scandinavian airline that had very nearly bought British Caledonian in the mid-1980s. Soon I was selling direct to airlines all over the world, cutting out the middle man, and was busy travelling and selling.

Gradually, we established ourselves as one of the world's leading aviation parts suppliers. We were expanding and we were thriving. I'd found my niche and I was soon able to hire a managing director to run Touchdown's UK office. Initially, America had been our biggest market but we had also developed our relationships with airlines in the Far East.

Although I had never wanted to store large quantities of material, it soon became inevitable and in 1999 we purchased a two-acre farm with a nineteenth-century farmhouse and two large warehouses on the outskirts of Badhoevedorp, right next to Schiphol Airport.

I set about turning some of the farm buildings into offices and building apartments for rent to offset the mortgage payment, while transforming the warehouses into state-of-the-art premises suitable for high-value aviation components. This included installing underfloor heating because spare parts do not like variations in temperature. The key thing was to avoid condensation because condensation equals corrosion, which you don't want.

We also built our own 'bonded' stores. This facility was kept under lock and key because all parts there were allowed to be fitted straight into an aircraft; we had been accredited the authority to certify them ourselves.

We called the property Julian's Farm. Fersam had been named after my eldest two children and I wanted to name our superb new premises after my youngest son.

Business was going very well. We were expanding. We were thriving.

And then two planes flew into the twin towers of the World Trade Centre in New York.

Chapter Twenty

SEPTEMBER 11

*It shall be lawful to any person, for the future,
to go out of our kingdom, and to return, safely
and securely – The Magna Carta, 1215*

I've always been in the habit of putting the television news on without sound while I'm working, allowing the images to form a flickering backdrop to whatever is going on in the office.

On this particular morning I was talking to a client in the Philippines from my office at Julian's Farm. The TV was on for the duration of the call and as I put the phone down I saw a commercial jet in a clear blue sky fly into an iconic Manhattan skyscraper.

In disbelief at what I thought I had seen, my first thought was 'this is trick photography'.

I put the volume up, still convinced it was a hoax.

And then as the camera focused on the first burning tower I watched as another airliner hit the second tower.

This was no trick and this was no accident. I was shocked, absolutely shocked. I called Patricia at home.

"Put the television on quickly," I said.

Within an hour and forty-two minutes both of the 110-storey towers of the World Trade Centre had collapsed. A third plane crashed into the Pentagon, the headquarters of the United States Department of Defence, in Virginia. A fourth plane was heading for Washington D.C., but came down in a field in Pennsylvania.

At that point everything went haywire. At 9.42am, fifty-six minutes after American Airlines Flight 11 had hit the North Tower, the Federal Aviation Administration grounded all civilian aircraft within the continental United States. Civilian aircraft already in flight were told to land immediately.

Within hours of the attacks, the FBI released the names of the suspected hijackers. Mohamed Atta, the ringleader of the hijackers, was the only Egyptian national among them.

The FBI confirmed that this was part of a series of four coordinated terrorist attacks by the Islamic terrorist group Al Qaeda. It soon emerged that large jets with long flight times had been selected for hijacking because they would be heavily fuelled.

For many days there were fears of further attacks.

This son of a bitch, Osama Bin Laden, not only killed more than three-thousand innocent people that day, he ruined the aviation industry, and he ruined safety and security between borders.

Every time I go through security at an airport, I condemn him. I say, "Damn you, Bin Laden, look what you've done to us all".

Before, there was always a rather bored-looking person chewing gum and glancing at the security cameras. No longer. Now airports are obsessional about security on an industrial scale, and check-in takes longer than ever.

It emerged that of the group of nineteen hijackers, only four knew they were not coming back. The others had been told they were going to fly the aircraft to Yemen and hold the passengers to ransom. The four pilots all had first class tickets and had taken knives through security with them.

It then emerged that they although they had learned to fly, they had only wanted to learn to navigate and to fly the plane in level flight – aspects that are not very technically demanding. Pilots earn their money when they touch down; getting the aircraft safely back on the ground is the challenge. But these men had had no interest in learning how to do that.

The owner of the flying club in Miami who had taught them to fly – unaware, of course, of their plans – had taken them up in a Cessna 172, a trainer that is a lovely aircraft to fly. Naturally, he was surprised to discover that learning to land did not interest them. And when the attacks in September 2001 took place he knew why.

As soon as 9/11 happened, everything stopped and business came to a standstill.

We got the first indication that the events of that day were going to affect us personally when the airports in the United States were closed.

Any plane that was in the mid-Atlantic was diverted to either Canada or to the Caribbean islands or into Mexico.

We had to stop and think; what were we going to do? Wall Street was closed and would remain so until 17th September. Civilian airspace did not re-open until 13th September.

As a commercial aircraft parts supplier we were facing big problems, and it was the same for all our competitors in this highly secure industry. There were no flights to America, and soon there was an understanding within the aviation industry in the United States that it would be advisable if spares were not purchased from overseas.

Everything was in turmoil.

Some of our American clients immediately started suspending their orders. We were also stopped from moving equipment because FedEx, UPS and DHL, with whom we had accounts to move our material, ceased shipping to the United States from Europe and the Far East. All the ports were also closed to foreign consignments.

The talk was that the terrible events of 9/11 were only the beginning and that there was a coming invasion of the United States.

The impact on business, to say nothing of the lives lost, was dramatic.

Overnight we lost about 70 per cent of our work.

During this time, I flew to Seattle with the manager of our UK office, to deal with a consignment of aircraft parts that, inevitably given recent events, had got tied up in red tape there.

We went at the end of October and the atmosphere in the airport was still very jittery and nervous. There was also a military presence there that I had never seen before in the United States.

And unfortunately, it was now very difficult with my Egyptian name, El Masry.

There were long delays; we were searched and frisked. My suitcase was held and I was left without a wash bag so I couldn't shave or do my teeth. It was frustrating but it was understandable; they had lost thousands of people and were worried they would lose more.

There are conspiracy theorists who know nothing about engineering, who claim that the twin towers of the World Trade Centre were detonated by United States government as a piece of propaganda. I don't believe this for a moment. The buildings were of steel construction and had been designed to be load-bearing on the outside of the structure only. The planes hit near the top of the towers. As the top floor fell it crushed into the floor below, which then fell with the combined weight of both floors. And on it went, in a horrific domino effect, as the steel structure unpeeled like a banana.

The compression was so intense that most of the metal changed state on a molecular level and became dust.

Things did not go back to normal after 9/11 for at least a couple of years. Customs were very thorough, paperwork was strict and there was more of it. Even when the restrictions eased up, we still had to take the time to describe in very detailed terms the form and function of the material in every box we were shipping. Frequently, the shipments were delayed at FedEx HQ in Memphis, Tennessee, because security checks there remained very strict. There was a sensation of great unease and everyone remained on edge for many months.

While all this was going on I was trying to work out a survival strategy. If the worst was to happen and I no longer had a spares business, how would I feed my family? Julian was nineteen and had only just started university. I had to find a way to make a living without the aircraft parts. Thankfully we didn't have a lot of staff back then as paying salaries for more than fifty people, as we do today, would have been impossible.

I decided to use all the spare cash I could lay my hands on to buy property to rent. Starting in 2002 I began buying apartments and renting them to companies – only companies; I did not want the stress of dealing with private individuals as my attention had to remain focused on the parts business once the apartments were up and running themselves.

At one point we had twenty-one properties with clients including Sony, Deloitte and DHL, although in time we went on to sell the majority of them. With the rent coming in I began to feel more relaxed about the future once again.

In 2008 I sold a number of high-value parts including

the *pièce de résistance*; a CF6-80A jet engine made by General Electric – a powerful turbofan engine that powers the Boeing 767 and Airbus A310, which both have two similar engines. The general rule of thumb is that the propulsion package on a twin-engine commercial airliner is about one-third of the total cost of the aircraft. I sold it for a handsome amount.

I celebrated by going on a shopping spree, buying a Bentley Arnage and a Nimbus speed boat; I'd already owned a couple of canal cruisers including 'Samantha' and 'Samantha Deux', both named after my daughter. I felt lucky to be alive to enjoy such lovely toys.

EPILOGUE

⁂

Spain, 2017

Gradually things got back to some semblance of normality in the slipstream that followed the terrible events of 11th September, 2001, and when they did TDA began to grow; new warehouses, more big deals with large operators, opening new offices in Europe, America and Asia.

By that time, my children Julian and Samantha were also working for the company. Two generations, side by side, running a family-owned business specialising in the supply, loan, exchange and repair of commercial aviation components.

I felt particularly proud that my youngest son, who had been born the same year that Fersam was formed, was now ready to become a part of our company.

Boy and business had grown up side by side, and by the age of fifteen, Julian had already developed an active interest in aircraft parts. He chose to use a lot of his free time after school and at weekends shadowing me and my staff, and gaining hands-on knowledge in the warehouse.

He knew at an early age that the company he had seen us build from scratch was something he wanted to be part of. He says that growing up with us has shown him the value of working hard, and playing hard as well.

And, after studying economics for three years at Vrije University in Amsterdam, Julian felt ready to join the company. In 2010, he became Managing Director at the age of just twenty-eight and assumed control of TDA's operations worldwide.

Dealing in aircraft parts – buying surplus stocks from the airlines themselves – had been the focus of our business for more than thirty years, but a few years ago everything began to change. Rather than buying large stores of surplus parts from the manufacturers of their fleets, such as Boeing or Airbus, many airlines began to buy only what they required as they needed it.

Worryingly, this meant that the potential for us to buy up surplus stock from the airlines began to diminish. Soon, even the major airlines began buying material from the surplus market. This meant we had a problem. Our supply line of parts from the airlines was drying up.

We needed to change tack, and we needed a new source of parts.

The answer lay in whole aircraft 'tear downs'. This is the process of buying a redundant aircraft and stripping it down for the parts we know we can sell on to the airlines for the right price.

Every year, 500-600 commercial passenger and freighter aircraft are withdrawn from service. The majority are disassembled.

In 2014 we acquired our first aircraft for tear-down – an ex-SAS Boeing 737-400. This represented a bright new future for the company, and this service then became the main focus of the business.

A Boeing 737 offers us between 650-700 high value items which we remove for service and re-sale.

The first thing we always do is try to sell the landing gear; on a £3.75 million plane, our sales people are generally able to achieve a six- or seven-figure price for this high-value component. Next, they find a buyer for the auxiliary power units – another six-figure price. By getting our sales guys to sell such 'hot' items as these first, we recoup our investment. After that, everything is profit. We generally buy planes without engines, known in the trade as 'donkeys', and which are generally a third of the cost of a new aircraft.

Once we've removed the key parts that we are interested in, we sell the rest for scrap. We don't want to deal with all the small bits and pieces. Selling the carcass, including the wings and the fuselage, is generally worth around £15,000 on the scrap market.

The down side of this new approach is that having spent my career trying my best not to acquire large numbers of spares, we now need to store a vast amount of material ready to ship worldwide at a moment's notice. This meant that as soon as Julian and I realised the tear-down market was the way forward, it was clear we were going to need more storage space so, in 2016, we bought a state-of-the-art warehouse facility in the Netherlands.

TDA's 125,000 square-foot headquarters is just a wingspan away from Amsterdam Schiphol Airport.

Together with our satellite offices and warehouses at London Gatwick, Miami and Singapore, we are now able to offer fast delivery of both routine and urgent aircraft parts worldwide at a moment's notice.

From being an aeronautical engineer working out of an Amsterdam cellar with piles of paper and a trusty telex machine, we are now one of the world's largest suppliers of commercial aircraft parts. We have grown into a business with a brilliant slogan devised by Julian that depicts the scale of our operations today; 'We're local. All over the world'.

The actual work of tearing down the planes we buy is carried out by professional organisations that are equipped to dismantle an aircraft. We use companies in Cardiff, Toulouse, Arizona, and Aragon in Spain.

Our current plan is to tear down twenty a year; we did seven in 2016.

But for all the sense of achievement this brings me, I find there is something bittersweet about the process. A plane is an engineering marvel. From the air-frame to the wings to the fuselage to the interior, these are beautiful pieces of technology. Each part has a place because it has a clearly defined function. A commercial jet is the perfect evolution of design. There is no redundancy – nothing extraneous or superfluous. Each gram counts when travelling close to the speed of sound.

So I sometimes feel that we are like vultures picking at these man made birds, and when they are relatively new it feels a bit regrettable.

In 2015, we tore down an aircraft that was only twelve years old at a facility in Wales. Manufactured in 2003, this Airbus A320 had logged just 40,000 hours flying for airlines including British Airways, GB Airways and EasyJet.

It was a great shame because commercial jets can fly three times that far.

But sometimes owners believe the sum of the parts is worth more than the revenue that could be obtained from continued operations.

In 2014, I went to see an Airbus that was even younger than that. The fuselage was unblemished and you could even read the part numbers on the skin. It had been leased to Air Asia by a company in Ireland. When Air Asia didn't pay, the lease company claimed it back and it went to a Thai airline who used it for two or three years before going bankrupt. The plane went back to the owners again and eventually they decided to claim off the insurance and sold it to us.

It costs a lot to keep an aircraft up to date with all its scheduled maintenance, so sometimes it can be more financially viable to sell. But in this case it was clearly flyable, even though it was destined never to take to the air again.

However, every cloud has a silver lining, and Julian likes to point out that tearing down such a new aircraft enables us to supply our customers with the latest generation A320 material, as opposed to the flooded market of vintage A320 components.

Around the time that Julian took over as Managing Director, Patricia retired and I semi-retired from TDA, although I remain its CEO. This was in large part due to my ill health. In the late 1990s, we had started spending much of the autumn and winter months in Portugal, then Spain, after I was diagnosed with COPD (chronic obstructive pulmonary disease). My lungs and airways are damaged, probably due to me having been a pipe smoker for much of my adult life, and cold temperatures make it worse. We still love the UK and Holland, but definitely only in warmer weather.

These days, Patricia and I spend a lot of time travelling between our homes and visiting our family. One of our greatest pleasures, like grandparents everywhere, is spending time with our growing families.

In 2015, Julian married his Dutch fiancée, Sharon, with whom he has our youngest grandchildren, Oliver and Kate, who were born in 2011 and 2013.

My daughter Samantha – known as Sammy within the family – is the mother of two fine boys, Thomas, fifteen, and Ruben, twelve, with her ex-husband, Colin Sietses, a colorectal surgeon.

When she is not looking after her boys, Sammy, who

NAZIE A. EL MASRY

studied Arts Management, Geology and History of Art at Vrije University, is Director of Operations at TDA. She initially joined Fersam – the company half named after her – in 1997.

We jokingly call Sammy 'The Dragon' because she is tenacious about ensuring none of the parts we sell is 'incident-related' – that is, she ensures it has the correct certification to prove that it has not been involved in a crash. There are always unscrupulous people trying to sell parts which should be legally scrapped, but Samantha never leaves a single stone unturned in her mission to rout them out.

Over the years I have been asked many times to supply parts for the military; can we find this or that? But I have always refused. We were a small company and couldn't afford a scandal, but more than that we refused to get involved in that world because Patricia and I believe war is a terrible thing, particularly for children.

We watched other companies going down that route and becoming a hundred times more successful than us, but we can sleep at night knowing that we did things in a morally correct way.

This extended to being careful about who we supplied. For instance, if you sell a component to Dubai you need to be aware that it might end up in

Sudan or Yemen, so we have always remained vigilant about who we deal with.

Being an independent, family-owned business has made TDA stand out from the rest and become the stable company it is today; something we are all very proud of.

As for Ferdy, he went his own way after studying law at Vrije University in Amsterdam, where he met his love. Last year Julian invited me for the evening to his London club, The Arts Club in Mayfair, to meet some business associates. In fact, he had arranged for his half-brother Ferdy to be there. It was very nice to see him.

Ferdy has grown up to become a successful lawyer and is currently a partner at Jones Day, an American law firm in London. In 2014, The Financial Times ranked him in the top ten at the Innovative Lawyers Awards in the UK and Europe for his cross-border approach to mergers and acquisitions; what Ferdinand calls "the cultural click". He called it "a proud moment" and he is cited yearly as being among the best corporate lawyers in the Netherlands. He has also lectured extensively at several notable law schools.

Ferdinand says his worst professional moment came during his first years in the Netherlands when you are required to litigate, which means you need to wear a toga. He was standing in court, pleading, and realised he was wearing a female colleague's coat instead.

"My mind was so focused on the case that I had not noticed the dark blue colour until I noticed it was a bit tight, and there I was in court with a raincoat. Standing there and seeing the judges had taken note of it, and everyone else around me, was horrific," he says. "Somehow, I managed to continue as if there was nothing wrong. An Oscar was in order."

As for the other members of my family, Uncle Youssef and I remained close and, both being Capricorns – famed for their ambition, determination and overachieving workaholism – in later life we got on very well indeed as friends and equals.

Sadly, Aunt Salma died of a heart attack in 1980 in front of her favourite store, Harrods. She was just about to board a taxi to take her home to Marble Arch after a shopping spree, when she collapsed on the pavement. Uncle Youssef, who died some years later at the age of seventy-two, was heartbroken as you would imagine.

In 2013, there was more sad news, when we were told that Soad, who had brought up Ferdy, Samantha and Julian, had also died of heart failure in Egypt at the age of sixty-eight while visiting her family. She was working for us until the very end of her life, and never learned to read or write. Although married, she never had children of her own and my children were always very important to her, as she was to them. Julian in particular adored her.

It was only after Soad's death that Patricia started cooking for us – until then, the kitchen had always been Soad's territory.

As for my elder sister Ragaa, she has experienced something of a liberation since the death of her husband, Adel, to whom she was married – rather unhappily – for nearly forty years. She is a very funny lady and always makes me laugh, more so now that she is a widow.

Her late husband was a biochemist with a military background, and he gave her hell. She had five servants in the house, yet he considered it was unacceptable for any of them to make him so much as a coffee; my sister had to do it for him. Adel was a very domineering character; Ragaa is highly intelligent and I believe he felt threatened by her independence. When she used to come and visit me he even used to try to stop her leaving their house in Heliopolis.

After he died, Ragaa came to stay with Patricia and me, and although she does not drink a lot, Ragaa does like Baileys with ice. As soon as I had poured her one, she lifted the glass and gave a winsome smile.

"Cheers, Adel, your health and thirty-eight years of misery!" And then she downed it in one.

She is very young at heart, like me. In fact, we both feel as if we are still in our twenties or thirties.

As for my brother, Nabil, we may have had our differences as children but we now talk every day. All his hard work as a teenager paid off when he became an eminent doctor and head of Tropical Diseases at NAMRU-3 (United States Naval Research Unit No. 3) just outside Cairo. This is one of the largest research laboratories in the North Africa-Middle East region.

It traces its origins to 1942, when American military scientists and technicians began working with Egyptian physicians under the auspices of the United States of America Typhus Commission. Following the Second World War, the Egyptian Government invited the U.S. Navy to continue collaborative studies of endemic tropical diseases with Egyptian scientists, and NAMRU-3 was formally established in 1946.

Dr Nabil Ayad El Masry worked there for the best part of thirty years. He was also part of the team that invented the radioactive tracer ink used in positron emission tomography (PET) scans.

Although we went through some tough times as children, owing to our very different personalities, we are able to sit and laugh about all this in later life.

And in 2005 I was lucky that my brother even changed my life.

In 2003, Patricia and I had gone on a cruise to Malta with two other couples from Badhoevedorp, our town in Holland. After the ship had docked, we'd gone ashore for a walk before deciding to return to our boat by horse and cart, which was great fun. Patricia noticed a horse-fly buzzing around my face but I brushed it away and took no notice as there were millions of them.

However, as soon as we arrived home I developed a severe case of 'flu. My entire body swelled up and soon the symptoms got serious; my sugar levels went through the roof and my kidneys began to shut down. I was in a mess. My GP sent me to hospital where blood tests were taken. A few days later I was diagnosed with Castleman's disease (CD), a rare condition which means there is an abnormal overgrowth of cells of the lymph system, a situation that is similar in many ways to cancer of the lymph nodes. Even though CD is not officially a cancer, it acts very much like lymphoma and can be fatal. And like lymphoma, it is often treated with chemotherapy without which I was told I might have only six to nine months to live.

I was given a form of liquid chemo, Valcyte, which led to a variety of alarming side effects.

I was devastated and set about putting my affairs in order. I made a will and I even purchased two burial places in Holland; for me, and for Patricia to join me in years to come. I was getting prepared.

And then, after fourteen months of this terrible uncertainty, my brother, the tropical diseases expert, came to visit. By this point I was convinced I was going to die.

He seemed troubled by the situation, and not only by the fact that his only brother had been given a terminal diagnosis. After scrutinising my medical history, he noticed that every four weeks my symptoms were particularly severe. In his learned way he thought that this might point to a parasitical infection transmitted by the Maltese horsefly I had encountered on holiday – this was an entirely different diagnosis.

Nabil spoke to Dr Peter Huygens, head of oncology at Vrije University hospital, who was treating me, and suggested that the chemo was stopped and I was put instead on a high dose of antibiotics.

In all, I stayed on antibiotics for ten weeks to ensure that the parasites, for that is what my learned brother thought they were, would leave my body for good.

Thanks to his intervention with some more high-dose antibiotics I am still here, like a bad penny. Touch wood.

Interestingly, the Dutch still believe I had Castleman's and I receive reminders from oncology for regular follow up blood tests, which I ignore. My family, being very religious, called it a miracle and if that is what it was, then I am glad.

I must say that I have rather lost faith in doctors now. When I contracted Lyme's Disease in 2016, after I was bitten by a tick during a game of tennis at our tennis club in Spain, it was my brother to whom I turned immediately for treatment.

Nabil himself has not been in the best of health in recent years. However, at the time of writing he is now eighty, and still has all his wits about him, sometimes giving lectures at The American University in Cairo.

Although I have always loved a challenge, after suffering Lyme's Disease I had a moment of self-doubt and found myself thinking, "Maybe I should get a rocking chair at home and go on little walks to feed the pigeons in the park". But I just cannot see myself doing that; I'd rather kill myself.

Although I gave up squash, my favourite sport, at the age of forty-nine, I don't feel old at all. At that age I was still playing for the first team at my club, but when they started calling me 'Grandfather' after the second or third game, I knew it was time to join the local tennis club.

Now, I play paddle tennis with guys who are in

their late thirties. I'm not as fast as they are, of course, but I can carry my own weight. I know I'm the weakest link, but I'm ready and I'm prepared for that. And that's why we end up with a good game.

Property has become a major distraction in retirement for me. I sold the doctor's surgery in 2007, but I still own and rent out Frisolaan.

Much of my time now is taken up with property development in Spain. My life has never stood still; I have always been on the go, and recently I thought it would be fun to build a house, having done a number of renovations.

So a couple of years ago we commissioned a beautiful art deco house cut into the cliff with a glass elevator and an infinity pool overlooking the Mediterranean, at our home in Altea, on Spain's Costa Blanca.

The late Spanish architect, Carlos Gilardi, was famous for building modernist houses which feature straight lines. I wanted curves. I was about to walk out of one of our initial meetings because he didn't think curves were his thing, when he changed his mind. The house was completed in 2014 and when he sent out his company Christmas card in 2015 it showed a photo of our house. Sadly, I think it was the only curvy house he ever designed because he fell off his boat and died the following year.

This year we are building a 5,000 square foot house in front of the first house. The new building, which has a sweeping 180 degree view of the sea, will also have an infinity pool. We have designed it to be half the size of our current ten-thousand square-foot residence, so it is more practical for the two of us. When the new house is finished we're going to move into it and I hope to build another one on the nearby cliffside as a commercial project. I really don't want to sit still.

Some people have suggested that I have become a property developer with this new interest, but I haven't. I will always remain an engineer at heart and that's the way I approach the creation of these demanding hillside houses. They are fun to do and must be done properly from a technical point of view.

When Patricia and I are alone together we choose to live quite quietly. She reads, and for some reason she likes to watch the same films over and over again. I watch with her until I can't bear it any longer and I'll say to her, "Shall I make something delicious?"

I'll then go downstairs and make a lovely tray of figs and fruits and cheese. And we sit together and eat. It's very companionable.

I continue to love going to airports, wherever we are. Of course I've witnessed it thousands of times, but seeing a modern plane take off remains a moment of absolute delight. I'm not a plane watcher but whenever I see a wide-bodied jet like a Boeing 747 rotating – that's the critical moment of no return when the pilot pulls the stick and the nose goes up and the thing takes to the air – I always call it a miracle. Even though I know the scientific principles, I still marvel that I am watching 350 tonnes of machinery apparently defying gravity.

Decades ago I used to go with my friend Trevor Adams to the end of the runway at Gatwick to watch the old Britannias with their four propellers take off fully laden en route to Nairobi. Back then it was a slightly different story. Whether they would actually make it was always touch and go. Sometimes they had to abandon take off because all three wheels had to leave the ground simultaneously, not with the nose up as with modern jet planes. And when at last we saw them successfully leave the ground, I used to thank God.

It was an achievement for them to be airborne.

In some ways, that feels like a metaphor for my life. Against all the odds, and despite numerous false starts, I never gave up and eventually I got airborne too.

In March this year Patricia and I flew to Amsterdam to celebrate our son Julian's thirty-fifth birthday. A few days later we were all due to travel on to Florida for a charity golf tournament sponsored by TDA. But first, I had an important announcement to make. We were half way through a light supper when I judged that the time was right to speak.

I put down my knife and fork, and cleared my throat.

"Julian, we are here to celebrate your birthday," I began. "We are both very proud of the man you have become. I am now seventy-four, and although I still feel young at heart I know I am not getting any younger. I feel that the time has come for me to hand the business over to you.

"As of today I am promoting you to the position of Vice President of TDA and Fersam International. I know you will do a wonderful job of looking after the entire business."

Smiling and looking slightly lost for words, a delighted Julian stood to hug me, and his mother, of course. We then raised a glass to his birthday and to his future success at the helm of the company we have all worked so hard to establish.

The following morning news of his appointment was emailed to all our staff worldwide. Congratulations soon flooded in from every part of our empire.

I had felt for some time that this was the next natural step for the business that Patricia and I had worked so hard to create. The thing about Julian is that he thinks like I do, and he consults me when there is a matter of importance. He seems always to know exactly how I would react in any situation.

He also has the same work ethic. With me there was never any such thing as "I'm on a lunch break". I worked when there was work to be done and I was always ready to wrap up a deal with our international clients, whatever the time of day. Julian does the same thing. He eats and sleeps the company.

If the phone rings in the middle of the night with an AOG (aircraft on ground), Julian doesn't baulk at going down to the warehouse himself to locate the crucial component without which the plane, wherever it is in the world, cannot fly. He will punch in the details of the required part to locate it, fetch it, and get it packed up ready for shipping first thing. He will do all this without thinking about the time, because it's in him; inside, as it was for me and Patricia.

Making our business was our life; we loved it and Julian is the same kind of man.

At the beginning I needed to hold the reins to ensure that things did not expand too rapidly, always mindful of the advice I was given by my father, as well as Dougie Goldstein and my Uncle Youssef. Do things small, do things slowly. If you do them slowly, you will do them better.

I did things ten times faster than my father who never liked surprises and, by his nature, Julian does things ten times faster than me. But as he has grown older, Julian has mellowed and absorbed the importance of slowing down a little as well. I am extremely proud of my son.

He and I have the sort of relationship that I never experienced growing up without a father, and which I would dearly have loved.

"It made a man out of you," my brother Nabil said recently, of the way I changed after our father died so suddenly and in such dramatic circumstances when I was twenty-four. Losing my own Ya Baba made me move on to the next step of my life. It woke me up, galvanised me into action and made me a more resilient man.

But for all my success I believe I have not changed all that much since this tragic early wake-up call during my early days in business. I have continued to persist in everything I have done. Whenever I have failed I have stood back up and tried again. At the beginning there were so many wrong turnings and dead ends, but I persevered. And with this attitude I began to realise that whenever a door closes, another one opens elsewhere. I believe you just have to remain determined enough to believe it is there and alert enough to find it.

When I last saw my father I was still known as the 'black sheep' of my family. If there is any sadness it is that my father didn't live to see the result of his unstinting belief in me, as I have with my own son.

However, I know he would be very proud of the man I have become, the business I have built and the strong and happy family I have made.

ACKNOWLEDGEMENTS

❧

Nazie A. El Masry

First of all, I would like to thank Jane Warren, my talented author, for enabling me to write this book. Jane's professionalism was a great asset that helped me remember my colourful life.

I am grateful to my son, Julian Marcus, who instigated the whole idea of putting my life down on paper. My daughter, Samantha Sietses El Masry, kindly helped research the pictures for the book.

I am lucky to count Angus Whiteside – the stepson of one of my mentors, Dougie Goldstein – as my longest and most loyal friend, who knows what I mean.

I remember with affection Arnold Sheead, who saw my potential in business and guided me throughout my career.

I am similarly indebted to my late uncle, Air

Commodore Youssef Wassef for looking after me in my student days.

And last but by no means least, thanks are due to my trouble and strife (my loving wife Patricia) who has been with me through thick and thin.

Finally, if you think this was an enjoyable read, just wait for the second edition.

Jane Warren

Thank you to Natalie Ayling for introducing me to Nazie and for your support throughout the project, and to Julian El Masry for commissioning the book and entrusting his father's colourful life story to me. Patricia El Masry was a generous hostess during my interview weekend at her home in Spain, while Nazie dealt with my many questions in person, and by email, with characteristic enthusiasm. Thanks are also due to David Thaxter who maintains www.british-caledonian.com, Toni Tingle at Mereo, Frank Brejcha for sharing his recollections, and to the family of the late Pete Lucas for allowing us to use the photograph of him and Arnold Sheead. I am grateful to Cheryl Stonehouse for proofreading the manuscript and indebted to Rozalia Sherwood of TravisBead.com for her extensive transcription work. Simon Worrall and Louise Dignand were my supporters throughout, and my children Bea Mulder and Willem Mulder were my inspiration. My contribution to this project is in memory of my mother Susan Warren.

Jane Warren is Senior Feature Writer at the Daily Express. She was Highly Commended in the 1993 British Press Awards and is the author of a number of books including The Ali Abbas Story (Harper Collins) and One Up; A Woman in Action with the SAS (Harper Collins) as well as A Self-Made Man (Hodder Headline) and Igor; The Courage of Chernobyl's Child (Boxtree).